With the Star of David
Through the Theresienstadt Hell

Memoirs of Dr. Viktor A. Pollak

ISBN 978-0-9686315-1-5

Congregation Agudas Israel
715 McKinnon Avenue
Saskatoon, Saskatchewaan
Canada S7H 2G2

CONTENTS

PREFACE   1

INTRODUCTION   3
  Postoloprty And Postelberg   5
  Hitler's Propaganda Plots   7
  Juden Raus!   7
  Hitler's Long Shadow   9
  Annexation of The Sudetenland   11
  Flight From Home   13
  Fatal Decision   15

ALONE IN PRAGUE   16
  In The "Dragon's Nest"   16
  Lost French Internship   17
  Second Chance   18
  Adventure In High Society   20
  Switching Universities   23
  A Brush With The Nuremberg Ordinance   25

THE ONSET OF THE "FINAL SOLUTION"   28
  My Apprenticeship   28
  Father's Watch   32

MY FRIEND BELA   34
  At Studies   34
  Bela's Wartime Adventures   37

BEFORE THE HELL GATES OPENED   41
  My Last Chance   41
  Good-Hearted Gestapo Guy   42
  Repressions Escalate   44

WELCOME TO THERESIENSTADT   46
  From Fortress To Gaol To Ghetto   46
  Theresienstadt - The Showcase Kz   49

SNAPSHOTS OF LIFE INSIDE THE WALLS   **51**
The Story Of A Lost Luggage   51
Pleasures Of Ss-Scharführer Heindl   58
Strategic Mica   63
The Man From Lodź   65
Minutes From Execution   67
How I Met My Dead Father   71

EVERYDAY GHETTO LIFE   **74**
News Seeps In And Around   74
A Christmas Gift   76
Well-Concealed Radio   79
Wedding   81
Starvation...   84
... And Illicit Pleasures   85
Census   87
Cameras   88
Health Care   89
Tangled Wires   90
Intrigue   94
Bullying   98
Dumpling   99
Into The Fire   100

BY THE SKIN OF THEIR TEETH   **103**
Fifteen Hundred Lives   103
Between Himmler And Göring   113
Last Minute Salvation   115

WHEN HELL WAS OVER   **118**
Booby Trap   118
Informative Documents   120
Drink To Comrade Stalin's Health!   122
Cruel Revenge   124
Senseless Death   126

EPILOGUE   **129**

FROM TEREZÍN TO SASKATOON   **130**

ACKNOWLEDGEMENTS

In the beginning, there was a manuscript of reminiscences and flashbacks taken down by Dr. Pollak many years ago. He first shared these memories by publishing excerpts in *The Bulletin*, the publication of Saskatoon Agudas Israel synagogue starting in 1993. The next step was the resolution of his wife Mirka to carry out her husband's wish to add the memoirs to innumerable testimonies of the Holocaust and atrocities committed by the Nazis against the Jewish populace in all occupied countries. They were published in his native Czech language in 2010. This was a long journey from the manuscript to this book considering that the author died in April, 1999.

The successful ending of this journey would not have been possible without several institutions and their staff to whom we want to express our acknowledgements for their helpful approach to this project, counselling, tips and illustrations:

Židovské museum v Praze (Jewish Museum in Prague),
Židovská obec v Brně (Jewish Community in Brno),
Archiv Památníku Terezín (Terezín Memorial Archives), Holocaust.cz,
United States Holocaust Memorial Museum in Washington .
LITTERA Publishing
Congregation Agudas Israel, Saskatoon, Saskatchewan, Canada

December 2014

PREFACE

More than half a century has past since the savage ideology of narcissism founded and implemented by Hitler and his cohorts, threw the whole world into turmoil, with disastrous consequences. When it finally ended, after only a dozen of the thousand years promised, more than fifty million people had died and most of Europe was in shambles. It is difficult to comprehend from today's vantage point the almost magical influence that man could exert over his compatriots. It forced them, with only a minimum of resistance, to disregard centuries of humanity and enlightenment and return to the savagery and disregard for human life which had prevailed during the darkest periods of the Middle Ages.

Like red thread, winding its way through the ropes of the rigging of the old sailing ships of the British navy, hate for anything foreign was the main tune of Hitler's preaching. Of course, one cannot hate everybody with equal intensity, as you cannot love several subjects equally. There has to be a degree, a progression. Number one on the Hitler's scale of hatred were the Jews. Jews were defined, not by religion, but by something labelled "race". Nobody was quite sure what that term really meant. Semitic Arabs were friends, but equally Semitic Jews were enemy number one. The reasons behind that pathological hatred are equally obscure. Many a psychologist has tried to find a rational explanation, but none of them have been successful. Also difficult to understand is the depth of anti-Jewish feelings Hitler was able to imbue in vast numbers of the population. There is no doubt that he had quite an unusual charisma. But charisma alone cannot explain his suggestive power, ot his ability to let a, by and large, well-educated population renege upon all principles of humanity and civilization.

Strange also is that so few of his followers perceived the worldwide contempt Hitler's ideology elicited, and that in the final event it would backfire and turn against their own country and cost uncountable numbers of lives of their own. Not perceived, nor even suspected by most, was that the preached contempt for humanity and human life directed initially against those undesirable sub-humans would inexorably spread to other populations and finally turn with equal fervour against them. That the slaughter of millions for no other reason than that they were imprudent enough to select parents who were not "racially pure" would only a few years later lead to the same disregard for the lives of the racially pure. The first to be sacrificed on the altar of Nazi ideology were millions of members of "inferior" enemy nations, followed by the lives of other millions of its own followers in the service of a doomed cause and to preserve the rule and the lives of its high priests for another few months.

This book brings the life story of a young man of Jewish descent, the author of this report, who was blind enough not to heed the signs on the wall before it was too late. He became, as many others with him, enmeshed in the deadly web of racial fanaticism and persecution. Fate was graceful to him. He managed to survive physically unharmed, though psychologically scarred for life. Nine times he was sentenced to death, and nine times he was spared; sometimes in the last minute. To have this happen nine times in a row is certainly not a common event. One might say it was the will of God, the hand of fate, a miracle or use any other designation. Whatever name you wish to give to that power, I am grateful for the additional decades of life I was granted. At the same time, I am deeply saddened when I remember the fate of the many relatives, friends, colleagues and fellows prisoners to whom that power was less gracious.

The context of this book covers mostly the years from the fall of Czechoslovakia until the end of the war. The episodes told, even the most unbelievable ones, are true. In the absence of written documentation from that period, I had largely to rely on memory. The reader will forgive me occasional lapses when my memory was failing. Virtually all episodes told in the following come from first hand experience. Only a few of them are second hand accounts. They are clearly identified as such. They were carefully selected from the many which came to my knowledge. Two main criteria were employed: absolute credibility of the source, and the event reported should fit into the general topic of this book - that is, to show how unexpected, unforeseeable events sometimes intervened to save a camp inmate from certain death.

Wherever possible, these reports were checked and compared with reports from other sources referring to the same place and the same time span. The names of the persons involved were generally altered in order not to intrude upon their privacy, especially in the case of persons still living at the time when I entrusted my memoirs to paper.

INTRODUCTION

I had a rather interesting life almost from the very beginning. My father, a lawyer, had long before World War I moved to Vienna, then the capital of the Habsburg monarchy of Austria-Hungary. The remainder of his family, three brothers, had remained in the small town of Postoloprty1 (Postelberg in German), in the northwestern part of Bohemia. I, the only child in the family, was born in Vienna in the second last year of the Great War. Of my mother, I don't know much more than her maiden name and that only from the inscription on my parents' tomb at the Central Cemetery of Vienna. I was less than a year old when my mother succumbed to the Spanish flu, which at that time raged all over the world where it claimed some 20 million victims.

My father, now alone, was not in the position to take care of a baby less than a year old. Therefore, I was given into the care of a sister of my mother's, a widow with two daughters several years older than I. Incidentally, she and one of the daughters perished in one of Hitler's death factories. Where and when exactly I could never find out. The other daughter managed to escape to Switzerland and survived. After the war, I searched for a decade or so, until I finally found her with the help of the Red Cross. After my escape from the then communist Czechoslovakia, I managed to meet her in Switzerland, but she was not happy to be reminded of her Jewish past. A few years after our short encounter, she died.

To come back to the years of my early childhood, my foster-mother was not very happy with the additional efforts and responsibilities caring for an infant imposed upon her. The war had in the meantime ended and there was a shortage of food and growing hunger in Vienna. In contrast, there was no shortage of food in Bohemia, which had recently become part of the new Czechoslovak Republic. Therefore, my father arranged for one of his brothers, who lived as a country doctor in the above-mentioned town of Postoloprty, to take care of me. It is more than 80 years since then. The

---

1 A distorted name of a Benedictine monastery Porta Apostolorum, founded there by the end of the 11th century. Postoloprty became a town in 1510.

shock I experienced as a four year old as I climbed from the train, which had brought me from the millions of people in Vienna to the few thousands of Postoloprty, is difficult to describe. There was hardly a house with more than two floors, some streets paved with cobblestones, no traffic jams, no policemen directing traffic, no street cars; in short, nothing of the amenities or nuisances of the big city.

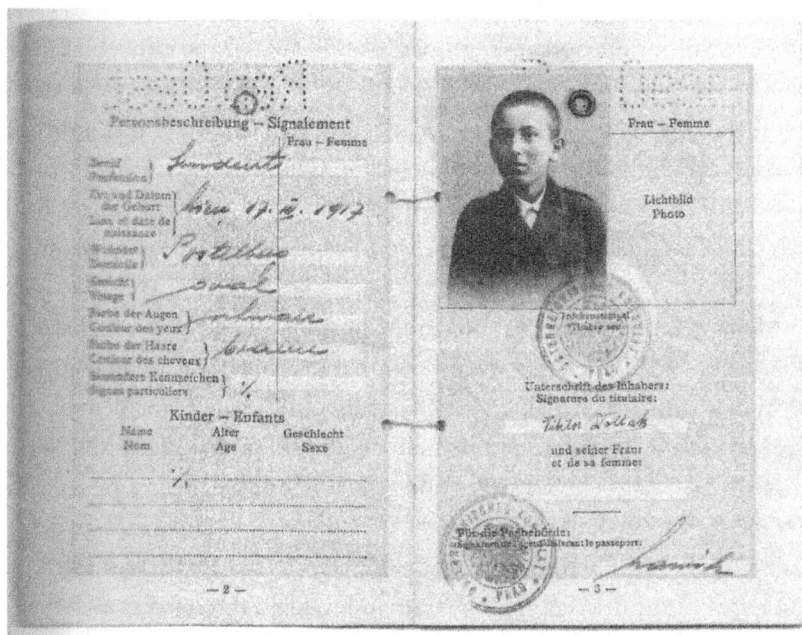

Picture: Viktor Pollak's passport, issued by the Austrian Consulate in Prague
(Photo archive of the Jewish Museum in Prague)

Postoloprty became my home for the following next two decades of my life. All my father's brothers were childless and they treated me as their own; I might even say they spoiled me too much. My father, who had stayed in Vienna, did not survive his wife's death for very long. When he died, I was adopted by my uncle and became a citizen of Czechoslovakia.

POSTOLOPRTY AND POSTELBERG

The town of Postoloprty was just at the language border. German was the dominant language spoken, but it also had a sizeable Czech minority and most people were, to use the Canadian term, bilingual. In spite of occasional frictions, the two language communities living side by side got along quite well. The town also had a Jewish community of a few hundred souls with its own synagogue in the "Jewish Street" and its own rabbi. Hostility against the Jews undoubtedly existed, but certainly not in the open. When you heard some derogatory opinions about Jews, they were usually phrased as "They, but not us..."

Illustrative picture: School in Postoloprty (scanned from the post card)

Born in Vienna, my mother tongue was obviously German. But that did not prevent me from having besides my circle of German buddies a handful of Czech friends. I attended the German elementary school in Postoloprty and then I took the daily train to the German high school in the neighbouring district town of Žatec (Saaz in German). Since there was no class in Jewish religion at that school, I took private lessons at the home of the local rabbi.

My adoptive father had plans for me to take over his medical practice. For that, of course, I had to get an education in medicine. Instead of waiting until university times, he taught me the basic vocabulary of medical terminology and gave me books from his extensive medical library to read. There was only a single automobile in town; it served as a taxicab and uncle hired it occasionally for his visits to patients in the countryside when the weather was especially bad. Most of the time we used a horse and buggy rented from a neighbour of ours. When I was not at school, I played the driver and also medical assistant. Sometimes when my uncle was out for a visit and I was at home, patients with some minor diseases, who had come from one of the villages in the surrounding countryside, asked to be seen by "the young doctor", as they called me. It seems ludicrous, but the experiences I had gathered at that time were put to good use in my career after the war.

I already mentioned that my uncle wanted me to take over his practice after his retirement. Of course, he did not anticipate the later course of events, which made that impossible. If I had followed his wishes, I probably would not be in the position to write these lines. My ashes would likely be toys for the river Ohře (Eger) or perhaps another river in Germany or Poland. Electronics and electronic communications were the subjects which attracted me and my uncle, though he did not like it, did not veto my intentions and permitted me to enroll after the completion of high school at the German Technical University of Prague, the capital of Czechoslovakia. I already at that time toyed with the, then definitely unorthodox, idea of joining electronics and medicine. My uncle had many connections to professors of the German Medical University of Prague and he got me permission to attend the initial years of medical studies at that University as an extraordinary student. I attended some classes there, unsure whether I should continue with engineering or switch over to medicine for good. Fortunately, as it turned out only a few years later, I could not stomach the extensive training in anatomy and the dissections which were part of it and decided to stick to my original intentions and stay with engineering.

HITLER'S PROPAGANDA PLOTS

Hitler's plans were at that time well crystallized and he started to implement them methodically step by step. He did not even try to any great length to conceal them and the only surprising circumstance is that the supposedly experienced and farsighted leaders of the Western powers were fooled by his ploys in the same way as the general population.

The opening salvo came from grinds of his propaganda machine. Its masterful general in chief was the Reich's minister of propaganda, Dr. Goebbels. With his clubfoot he had been given, by those who were less his friends, the nickname "the hobbling Lucifer". His initial barrage was aimed at the German speaking population of the Sudeten and he accomplished this with astonishing success. The episode outlined in the next two paragraphs is an example of its effectiveness.

JUDEN RAUS!

It was late summer in 1938 and I had for the summer vacations returned from Prague, where I was attending the German Technical University, to Postoloprty, the small, sleepy country town in northwest Bohemia where my adoptive parents spoiled me, as if I had been their own child. Of course we read in the newspaper about the events which were taking place in Germany, less than a hundred kilometres north across the border. We also read about the persecution of Jews there, about the pogroms of the "crystal night" and other horror stories. However, we believed that the newspapers were exaggerating. Only later we learned that just the opposite was true, and that what we were told was rather an understatement of the truth. Perhaps we simply did not want to know the truth, perhaps we felt secure by the heavily guarded border, which separated us from the colossus in the north. Most of the hundred or so souls of the Jewish community in our town had been brought up with a German cultural background and perhaps they could not believe that the nation of Goethe and Schiller would be capable of endorsing the hate-inspired ideology of National Socialism, as it euphemistically called itself.

Anyway, for whatever reasons, nobody in the community felt threatened by the development of our neighbours. That feeling of safety, of security, developed some cracks withthe emergence of the Henlein movement. Konrad Henlein was a surrogate of Hitler for Czechoslovakia, and the movement he headed was a true copy of the original NSDAP (the acronym for the German Nazi party[2]). The Henlein movement spread like wildfire through the German part of Czechoslovakia. Though everybody knew that Henlein was just a proxy for Hitler, not even that caused real fear or serious anxiety in our community. For me the real shock came in June that year.

Picture: Pollak's (VP marked "X") class at Žatec gymnasium
(Photo archive of the Jewish Museum in Prague)

Before going to University in Prague, I had attended the German language high school (State German Natural Science Gymnasium) in the neighbouring district capital of Saaz. I had not visited the school for quite some time and so I decided to drop by one day. I arrived just at the time of intercession and the students were frolicking around in the corridor just

[2] Nationalsocialistische Deutsche Arbeiterpartei

as they had done before, during my school years. On the surface, nothing seemed to have changed. But there was change in the atmosphere. Though I still knew quite a few of the upper class students from my own school years, and they undoubtedly knew me, no one talked to me. I was ignored by everybody as if I had been a complete stranger. Finally, by chance, I met my former professor of mathematics and physics. We had an excellent relationship in the old years. I had been one of his favoured students and at the final exams he had awarded me the rather uncommon degree of special distinction in Natural Sciences. However on the day of my visit, he was quite different, strange and cold as ice. He pulled me into a corner, where we were somewhat out of sight, and in a low voice he told me to disappear as fast as I possibly could, otherwise my safety would be in jeopardy. As a special favour, for my security, he would accompany me to the main entrance. There we would part without a handshake and I should never come back. And I never did in the near sixty years that have elapsed since then. It was the first warning of things to come. Unfortunately, the significance of that warning failed to sink in.

HITLER'S LONG SHADOW

Postoloprty, the small town I was talking about before, was just at the border between the Czech speaking bulk of the population of Bohemia and the Sudetenland at the Northwest where the German language dominated. In the town itself, the German language prevailed, but relations with the sizeable Czech minority were by and large good and peaceful. The town had a Jewish community with its own synagogue and rabbi. Most, if not all of the local Jews considered themselves Germans and their children, me included, went to the local German grammar school. That conciliatory state of affairs lasted until the rise of Nazism, when Hitler's puppet Henlein taught them better.

An episode, which brought the recognition of the growing change starkly home to me, was the reception I was given at a visit to my former high school in Žatec, during my university summer holidays of 1938.

Many of the changes, caused by the Hitler regime, to the old character of

Postoloprty persist today. The old inhabitants, to the extent they are alive, are dispersed all over Europe. Most of the Jewish population fell victim to the gas chambers in Auschwitz or perished from the suffering in other camps. The few that escaped in time or were lucky to survive the death camps are dispersed all over the globe. The synagogue is in ashes and the place where it once stood, an empty field. The Jewish cemetery is not there anymore. The tombstones, some of them centuries old, are gone. What happened to the bones I do not know. A children's playground was to take its place. But during my occasional visits after the war to the town, which had been home to my youth, I have never seen a child playing there.

Our neighbour in Postoloprty was a judge, a German. He had a son a few years younger than me, but we were nonetheless playfellows and you may say even friends. One day, when the Czechoslovak army had been mobilized and positioned in the chain of fortifications along the German frontier, the two of us had afternoon coffee in the judge's house. Erwin was the boy's name, and he expressed vehemently the hope that the German army, supposedly massed just across the border, would overrun the Czech army in no time and "liberate" the "oppressed" German people in the Sudetenland. At that time, we still relied upon the alliance with France and England and the protection it promised. I told Erwin, "true, the Czech army is no match for the German, but an attack would bring Western Allies into the play and the resulting large scale war might easily cost millions of lives." His answer was, "What does it matter? It is the price one has to pay for freedom. I will be happy to sacrifice my life for the Führer, Fatherland, and Freedom."

It was the last time we met. After the occupation of the Sudeten by Hitler, Erwin was drafted into the army. Somewhere in the East, I don't know when and where, he was wounded, lost his eye and was crippled. He survived the war just long enough to experience the destruction of the regime of his adored Führer.

ANNEXATION OF THE SUDETENLAND

As the thirties were tending towards their end, Hitler was busy rearming Germany. In the earlier part of the decade, he had managed to establish himself as the Führer, the absolute master of Germany's fate and his cohorts of the Gestapo and SS as the vigilant executors of his will. Not that there was much of an opposition among the German populace. Armament money was flowing in streams and gave the impression of a flourishing economy. Unemployment was as good as nonexistent and carefully cultivated hatred against the Jews, the sources of all the misery, which had befallen Germany in the years after World War I, proved to be an efficient focal point for people's emotions. At this stage, Hitler began to turn his eyes openly towards the exterior. Not that this was a secret. Everybody who took the pains of reading the Nazi bible, *Mein Kampf*, could have found it out because the book's author had made no effort to conceal his intentions. But the leaders of the democratic countries tired of the sufferings the previous war, though victorious had inflicted upon their nations. It was this attitude that prevented them from stopping Hitler, when it could still be done at minimal cost. Hitler was clever, he employed a step-by-step approach; each step too small to trigger outright response from his neighbours. Remilitarisation of the Rhine provinces was the first step. When that did not elicit much of a response, Czechoslovakia became his next target.

Czechoslovakia was anxiously watching the negotiations of its allies while Hitler was preparing for war, a war that, without foreign help, would have been lost from the beginning. Czechoslovak troops were concentrated at the heavily fortified belt facing the anticipated roads of intrusion of the invaders. A lieutenant colonel of the defending unit was billeted in our house in Postoloprty and he did not keep his information about the progress of the negotiations from us. After a week or so of uncertainty he took leave of us, announcing that the troops had orders to retreat behind a demarcation line and that the area beyond that line, our town included, would be occupied by the Wehrmacht. He did not reveal any secrets. The next day the dreaded news was in the papers and dates and all details warning all those who had reason to be afraid of Nazi occupation to flee into the Czech mainland.

I had spent my summer vacations from university in Postoloprty, which

I had come to consider my hometown. Radio was not a common device at that time, but I was deeply interested in the secrets of invisible waves propagating over hundreds of miles and carrying messages, which could be retrieved at locations far from the place where they originated. I had managed to build a receiver, primitive even according to the standards of the time, but it enabled me to listen not only to the Czech broadcast, but also to the stream of Nazi propaganda intended for Henlein's followers. I was only too well aware of the hate against Jews these transmissions were spreading.

When we learned of the imminent occupation by Nazi troops, I had no illusion about the life that a Jew could expect to live in Hitler's shadow. Admittedly, I did not even dream of the future horrors of Dachau, Mauthausen, Majdanek or Auschwitz, but that little I knew was sufficient to convince me that flight was the only choice.

It was in September 1938, when Britain and France made their last attempt to appease Hitler, who was supported by the Italian dictator Mussolini. Tense negotiations took place in Munich. The leading spokesman at the Allied side of the table was British Prime Minister Neville Chamberlain. We had given him the nickname, "the umbrella man", because of the umbrella at his side in all his pictures. He wanted to avoid an armed conflict with Germany at whatever cost and had an almost naïve trust in Hitler's sincerity. We know today that at that time, Germany was not ready for war, and Hitler, knowing this, would almost certainly have given in if his bluff had been called. Whether Mr. Chamberlain was misinformed by his intelligence service or whether it was political opportunism that caused him to override the report of his intelligence service, I do not know. What we do know is that he trusted Hitler's word that Czechoslovakia was the last of his territorial aspirations and that he was prepared to pay the price Hitler demanded. The price to prevent a large-scale war was agreement to the "peaceful" annexation of the Sudetenland by Hitler's Germany. The infamous agreement was signed at Munich in September 1938, and the Czechoslovak government had to surrender Sudetenland, the border territories of Bohemia and Moravia with its mainly German speaking population, to the Reich. That Hitler had deceived the Allied leaders into believing that he had no further territorial aspirations became obvious only a few months later, in March 1939.

FLIGHT FROM HOME

The German army crossed the border, with the Gestapo and the SS in its tow, in October 1938. The Czechoslovak army, vastly outnumbered and left alone by its allies, was ordered to retreat from its fortified lines and take up new positions behind the new border. These movements took some time and gave us a few days warning. For me the decision was clear, though it involved some trust into Hitler's promise that he would leave the remaining rump of Czechoslovakia alone and unmolested, because he ostensibly did not want a sizable chunk of the population of non-German nationality. In that I was wrong, as soon became evident.

On the other hand, to stay would have been worse and more dangerous. The only immediate response to the situation seemed to move permanently across the new border to Prague. The problem was my uncle and aunt. I begged them to come with me. My uncle refused, saying that he had never done harm to anybody, that he had always considered himself German rather than Czech, and that he had no enemies, neither Czech nor German. What he did not see was that in the eyes of the Nazis he was neither Czech nor German, just a Jew. Alas, he underestimated the intensity and the spread of the infection of the Nazi disease and the opportunism of many of those he believed to be his friends. He also failed to appreciate the sheer terror the Nazi regime was wielding, and the efficiency of the organization that carried it out. No argument, no persuasion could shake his decision not to leave. Auntie supported my intention to go to Prague but said she could not leave my uncle alone. With a heavy heart, I realized I could not shake my uncle's decision and that I would have to go my own way. To stay in Nazi country seemed to me to be close to suicide. I found out only much later how close my thoughts were to reality.

My adoptive parents and I spent virtually the whole night discussing our options. My decision was already made and I tried to convince my uncle and aunt to go with me, but my uncle objected, "I have treated the Germans and Czechs alike and I don't think that I have any enemies in either nationality. And from what will we live there? You know I am too old to open a new practice anywhere else, even if I were allowed to do so. And I don't think my pension would be transferred to Prague." I had to admit that his objections were serious, but I insisted that we would handle the situation in one way or another. My uncle said he would prefer me to stay with him and my auntie, but if I decided to flee, he would not object.

Come the morning, nothing had been decided yet. We kept debating and arguing. It was perhaps 9 a.m. when a friend of ours, Mrs. Müller walked in. Mrs. Müller was the owner and operator of a small textile shop in the main square. She had many friends on both sides of the language barrier and had been warned emphatically to leave as long as there was still time. She had guessed what was going on at our place and the quandary I was in and had come to help me.

She flatly declared that the last train was supposed to leave at 2 p.m. and asked that I pack up my suitcase as fast as I can. She definitely had no intent to miss the last train before the arrival of the Wehrmacht. Time was more than tight. She said she would come after lunchtime to pick me up and accompany me to Prague. In Prague, we would separate and go our own ways. She would go to her sister in Příbram, and I would stay at my lodging.

She joined me in trying to persuade my uncle, but in vain. My uncle declared that he felt safe even under German occupation and that he would not leave. Auntie had no such conviction, after all she was of Czech extraction, but she insisted that she would not desert my uncle at the crossroad of fate. My decision to flee had become somewhat shaky in response to my uncle's arguments, but Mrs. Müller resolutely declared, "You come with me." That decided the matter. My suitcase was almost packed and only a few things had to be added. Mrs. Müller was afraid I might still change my mind, so she stayed until everything was prepared

As arranged, she picked me up shortly after lunch and I said goodbye to my uncle and auntie, never to see them alive again.

Mrs. Müller, with me in tow, made it safely to the train station and even managed to occupy two seats in the over-crowded train. The train, the last train before the separation of the Sudetenland, was crowded to the last centimetre of floor space. All the luggage I had was a suitcase, a foreshadow of my voyage to Theresienstadt a few years later.

The train was slow, very slow. The travel to Prague, which normally took a little more than two hours, took this time the remainder of the day. On route, we had many stops where trains with troops and war material passed us. We arrived in Prague, the capital, shortly after midnight. The train was not that crowded anymore. Many of the refugees had left the train at different places before we arrived at the capital.

In the park in front of the Main station, I took my leave of Mrs. Müller. As already mentioned, she planned to go to Příbram by the next train. How she made it, I don't know. She did not stay with her sister and I never saw her again. Nor do I know her fate.

FATAL DECISION

My uncle had been wrong in his assessment of the future under Hitler. For a couple of months things seemed to go reasonably well. Although they were publicly ostracised and subjected to all kinds of discrimination, some people, mostly Germans as virtually all Czechs had fled, came at night (in the daytime they were too afraid), bringing butter, milk, and other food that my uncle and aunt, as Jews, were prohibited from buying. The things they brought were left in the grass at the back of the house. However, the situation soon became worse. The nightly visits became fewer and fewer. Then my auntie died, from what cause I never found out. She could not be buried in the Jewish cemetery of the town. Instead, her body was moved to a field some twenty miles away, which was made the only burial place for Jews in the region. The grave sites were unmarked and shortly before the end of the war, the whole "cemetery" was ploughed under.

My uncle was sent to a local camp at Edersgrün (Odeř in Czech) near the famous spa of Karlovy Vary. From there he was later deported together with a Jewish farmer from the same town who had made the same mistake as my uncle, to the Theresienstadt[3] ghetto, where they both arrived dead, cause of death unknown. t that time I was already an inmate of that camp, and was allowed to see my stepfather's corpse for a few minutes.

---

[3] The name of the town has been Terezín since the end of the WWI. Here, it is called Theresienstadt, its German equivalent, when the ghetto period is meant.

ALONE IN PRAGUE

IN THE "DRAGON'S NEST"

I had to get to my student lodging from the Main Station, and because I could not squeeze with my suitcase into any of the full trams, I had to make my way on foot. Many of the other refugees were less lucky, they had nowhere to go. All hotels, pensions and the like were filled to the brim with people sleeping in lobbies and corridors on blankets or cots. In the arrival hall of the station, there was hardly a place not occupied by a refugee family and their luggage. Though the night was quite cool already, all benches and all lawns in the park in front of the station were occupied.

The next morning I found out that further troubles lay ahead. My room belonged to a remote cousin of my aunt and her husband. Though they tried hard to avoid the appearance of being Jewish, it did not help much. Everybody knew they were Jews, also their landlord was a German. The first thing he did after Munich was give them notice, so that his house would be clean of Jews. They had to look for a new apartment. Since the one they finally found was too small, I had to look for some accommodation for myself.

With some help from friends and colleagues, I found one in a Jewish house in one of the suburbs. The apartment where I found a room belonged to an old lady who went by the nickname "the dragon". On the ground floor of the same house lived the family of another refugee, a former textile merchant from the well-known spa of Mariánské Lázně (Marienbad). The family had two daughters: one almost a child, the other one in the her late teens.

It was not long until a curfew was imposed upon Jews, forbidding them to leave their place of residence after 8 p.m.[4] And so it was almost inevitable

---

[4] Since 1 September 1939

that the older daughter of my neighbours and I became, first friends and then, lovers. A couple of years later she became my "ghetto wife".

I lived in that house until late 1941, when my "dragon" landlady was deported to the ghetto of Lodź in Poland never to be heard of again. The apartment was confiscated and given to a German officer. I had to look for another place to stay. However, for a Jew to find such a place, let alone social connexions, was far from easy. Fortunately, I got help from some non-Jewish friends. One of them did a good job indeed.

In the apartment of my aunt's cousin, where I had stayed during my previous student years, was another student, the son of a wealthy Polish family from Lodź, Mr. K. He was more interested in sports than in studies and, being an excellent tennis player, had joined the predominantly German tennis club LTC. Somehow, he had arranged that I be admitted into this exclusive club and meet many people from the high society. I believe they sympathised with me, and most of them liked me.

When the Protectorate of Bohemia and Moravia was established, I was expelled from the club and everyone publicly ignored me. In private, however, it was different and if there was no danger of public exposure, many tried to help however they could. And it was with help from them, and after considerable effort, I succeeded in finding a room. True, it was small, miserably equipped, and expensive, but I had no choice. It had just a washbasin with cold water and the toilet was on the corridor, common with the other tenants on the same floor. After all, this was not unusual at the time and many of the old houses of the city were no different. I stayed in that place until February 1942, when I got that fateful order of deportation to the, then new, ghetto Theresienstadt.

LOST FRENCH INTERNSHIP

During my studies in Prague, I attended L'Institut français and gained a reasonable fluency in the French language. France was, at that time, regarded as the principal friend and ally of Czechoslovakia. The Institute was actually financed by the French government. Its main mission was to propagate French culture and language and to enhance friendly relations between the youth of both countries. After three years of attendance, I passed an exam and was awarded a three months' internship to spend at a hydro plant in the French Alps. It would have been my first opportunity to travel abroad since as a four year old I had travelled from my birth city of Vienna to Czechoslovakia. I perhaps do not have to stress the excitement I felt. At the same time, there was a feeling of uneasiness I found hard to explain. Then fate intervened with consequences, which at that time could not even be guessed.

Near the town of Postoloprty flows a moderately sized river, the Ohře. In summer the town maintained a public bathing facility, which was very much favoured by the youth of the town, myself included. The river was quite deep in places and I loved to dive and to swim under water. I am, and was, short-sighted and had to wear special glasses. Normally one takes their glasses off when diving, but for one reason or another, on one of these days I neglected to do so. My glasses fell off and sank to the muddy bottom. All efforts to recover them were futile and I did not have spare glasses. To get a replacement would have taken a couple of weeks and I was afraid to travel into the unknown virtually blind. The deadline for my travel to France was set, and efforts to postpone it were unsuccessful and the opportunity was lost. For better or the worse, who knows? Sometimes I reflect on what would have happened if I had not lost my glasses. Would I have stayed in Paris until the German invasion, with almost certain death the consequence? Would I have managed to go to England where, in all likelihood, I would have joined the army? Would I have managed to escape to the U.S. to return with Eisenhower's army? It is hard to say. A small event, the loss of my eyeglasses, changed the whole course of my life.

SECOND CHANCE

An opportunity missed is an opportunity lost. This is the rule of life and exceptions to that rule are rare. This was one of the rare exceptions. Fate offered me a second chance only to also take it away in the last moment.

A remote cousin of mine, a well known architect, had developed a courageous and avant-garde design for a bridge, which was to span the broad valley which divides the main body of the capital city of Prague from its southern suburbs. A model of that bridge was to be displayed at the world exhibition, which was scheduled to be opened in Paris in the near future. The model was to be made from transparent plastic and a special optical system was to visualize the distribution and the trajectories of the lines of tension in the bridge material with streetcars, autos, and buses passing over it. I was to design part of that fairly complex system and as a reward was promised a position as guide on that part of the exhibition. That promise was tied to a condition: reasonable fluency in French. In order to meet the condition I was training hard and diligently to polish up my French.

I was living now in Prague, attending University. To the extent I remember, my architect-cousin who had a Jewish wife had found his position in Paris too precarious. He had accepted an invitation to the U.S. and taken the next available boat to New York. His wife and children had stayed behind in Prague and his main concern was now to bring them to the U.S. He succeeded, but my fate understandably became the least of his concerns. At least my application for a French visa was not cancelled and was still running. I do not have to explain that I felt like I was on a bed of thorns, checking the mail impatiently day-by-day, hoping for a letter from the French consulate with the longed for visa approval. Nothing came and all interventions at the consulate produced only a shrug of the shoulders. In the meantime, a year had gone by. There were university holidays, which I spent at the home of Mrs. Charvát in Příbram, a medium sized mining town some eighty kilometres south of Prague. I had somehow arranged mail delivery for the time of my stay there. I remember as if it were today, the last weekday in August. A letter arrived with the stamp of the French consulate in Prague on the envelope. I jumped on it, but then was hesitant to open it, my mind vacillating between hope and resignation. Finally, I got myself to open it and there it was - a terse message that my visa had been granted and I could pick it up on presentation of a valid passport at the consulate during regular business hours. I, fortunately had a valid passport and so the next day I took an early morning train to Prague. Arriving at the main station, I made my way to the French consulate which was located quite far from the station, in the old historic part of the city. When I got there, I was in for a shock. Police cordoned off the square where the consulate was located. Hundreds of people were milling around, but nobody was allowed to pass. The wildest rumours were swirling around but they finally crystallized around some apparent facts: Germany was invading Poland, and the consulate was packing and about to depart. I did not get my visa and the next day France was at war with Germany.

ADVENTURE IN HIGH SOCIETY

At the time of my escape to Prague, I was a spoiled brat who in almost everything relied upon the help and advice of his adoptive parents. All of a sudden, I was cut off from them and had to make all relevant decisions all myself. Fortunately, the transition to this stage came gradually, my aunt's relatives and friends were helping me.

I have mentioned Mr. K., whose family owned a textile factory in Lodź. He brought from his hometown, not only plenty of money, but also connections to the top echelons of Prague's elite society. There were few, if any, language conflicts in that group. Germans, Slovaks, Czechs and even some Jews mingled there freely. Mr. K. was more interested in sport, social contacts, girls, and parties; studies were only a sideline. As an excellent tennis player, he had joined the tennis club with courts on the Letná heights overlooking the Vltava River, which divides the city of Prague in half.

Although membership of the club at the time was predominantly German, that did not prevent the president of the city police, a judge of the Supreme Court, and above all Mr. Hácha, later figure president of the Protectorate under German occupation, and many other top figures of the Czech high society from being club members. To join, you had to be recommended by at least two members in good standing. With the pocket money I was receiving from home, membership fees were quite out of my reach. I didn't stand a chance. My colleague knew that I enjoyed tennis and in part to give me access to high society circles, arranged for me to join the club as a "promising young player". As such, I not only did not have to pay any fees, but also was given free balls, rackets and six hours a week training under the guidance of the top players of the club. The young players, boys and girls, were also expected to be at the service of their guardian angels, who were older members of the club. What services were expected of me I found out only later. An episode featuring a rather delicate subject occurred, which explains it quite well.

One day in late fall 1938, I had been playing late, almost until darkness fell. Electric lighting was available only at the centre court and only for a few of the top players. My partner was a pretty woman, perhaps a decade and a half older than I. She was the wife of the owner of a metal handling company and to say that they were well-off would be an understatement. The family acted as a kind of sponsor for me and I was in turn expected to help her polish her game. After the game, I accompanied her to the main building of the club where I usually took my leave to return to the separate building for a shower and change. Not this time.

At the entrance to the main building she said, "Thanks for the nice game we had. You probably have not seen the seniors' building. Come, I'll show it to you. I am sure you'll find it interesting."

A security guard was stationed at the entrance to the main building and would have normally prevented me from entering, because the building was the exclusive domain of the club's full members. But in the company of that lady he let me pass without saying a word. My companion brought me to a shower cabinet saying:

"Take a shower now. I'll shower too. You wait here until I pick you up."

"But all my street clothes are in the other building."

"No matter, you can take a house coat; there are plenty of them in the shower cabinet."

Though I was somewhat apprehensive, I followed her instructions. When I came out of the shower, my tennis shorts were gone but a sumptuous bath coat lay there prepared and, like it or not, I had to put it on. My sparring partner had not yet returned so, following her instructions, I made myself comfortable while waiting for her.

She finally came, dressed only in a bathrobe similar to mine but made from a semi-transparent fabric, which did not do much to conceal the secrets of her luscious body. She sat on the bench close to me. I moved a few inches away. In vain. She moved after me, pressing her body even closer to mine. I can't say I disliked her initiative. I was young and this was an entirely new experience. It occurred to me only later that this was the test of a "promising young player".

After a while, she said calmly, "It was great, but you have a lot to learn. Now stay here and wait until I come back. I'll introduce you then to the crowd."

With that she left, leaving me alone in the antechamber of the shower room. I had heard rumours of these and similar events before, but I had not given them much credence. Now, when reality seemed to confirm them, I did not know how to react. To sum up, I was pleasantly excited, but at the same time afraid. It took the lady half an hour or so before she came back, now fully dressed. She brought my tennis dress, which she had obviously removed whilst I was in the shower, complemented by a white tennis jacket, which had not been part of my outfit.

She led me to a small table where two more of the "promising young players" group were sitting. They were like me, clothed in white tennis dress, whilst the remainder of the people in the hall had formal evening dress, tuxedos and tailcoats for the men, long evening gowns for the women. There may have been some twenty-five persons altogether.

A sumptuous dinner was served, with wine, beer, and liquors of choice. Then the room went dark, and only a small stage at one end of the hall was illuminated. Then three young girls came marching in, stark naked. There were three leather-covered broad benches on the stage and the girls, who obviously knew the drill, lay down. We did not know the routine, so we watched preparatory procedures, which I prefer to leave out.

When the female cast was ready, one of the club's bosses came to our table and asked us to follow him. He brought us into a small room behind the stage where he asked us to undress and then led us to the stage. The floor of the stage was covered with a soft high pile carpet and we had to lie down on it. A perfect staging.

Then a call rang out: "Group one into action!"

A group of six people, men and women, came forward mounting the stairs that went up to the stage, all clad only in their underwear. These were perhaps participants from the ranks of high society, willing to "entertain" themselves and others. I don't know whether the girls were professionals. We, promising players, were definitely amateurs, although for two of my colleagues this was certainly not the first acting in this place. Most of the people in the room, men as well as women, were crowding at the foot of the stage, intently watching every detail of the show.

I did not follow other guys, but when I finished my part, they took me to the bathroom to have a shower. Then I was given a not too subtle hint that my presence was no longer desirable. I went home, rather shaken up, and it took some time before the events of that evening faded from my memory.

SWITCHING UNIVERSITIES

At home, we had almost exclusively been using the German language, though my auntie came from a Czech-Jewish family and was fluent in both languages. My education (primary school, high school and the first two years of university) had all been in German. Though I knew some Czech, my knowledge of the language was rather poor. Uncle was a country physician and would have liked nothing better than for me to study medicine and take over his practice. However, he had not counted on the hard head of his nephew, who had made up his mind to study electronics. Electronics as a separate field then did not exist but was part of electrical engineering. Therefore, I enrolled in that field at the German Technical University of Prague.

There had been no problems during the first two years, although everybody knew that I was Jewish and in spite of the fact that the Henlein brand of Nazi ideology had during that time all but swept the German population. For the time being I had not experienced any curiosity or discrimination, perhaps with the exception of one professor, Dr. N., who long before did not conceal his views that Jews ranked way below even the lowest member of the animal kingdom. Now my relatively benign situation began to change fast.

After my arrival at Prague, when I showed up at the University, my fellow students, even those who had been more than friendly, took pains to distance themselves to show that I did not belong with them. It did not take long before I got a formal letter from the University that my attendance at lectures and seminars was not desirable anymore, that my matriculation was cancelled and that I should no more consider myself a student of the University. I had more or less expected that development, but when I had it officially, black on white, it nonetheless came as a shock. What to do now? The idea to switch to the Czech Technical University had occurred to me before and now I tried to implement it. This turned out to be far from easy. That resentments regarding my former German enrolment would exist, I could expect. These sentiments were aggravated by the fact that I was Jewish, and the anti-Jewish feelings propagated by the Germans had had its effects here; combined with, and intensified by, the growing animosity against anything German. The latter feelings could not be shown publicly, of course. The opportunity to combine forbidden anti-German sentiments with allowed and even supported anti-Jewish feelings was a Godsend. It happened as it was expected to. My application for admission at the Czech Technical University was refused and refused and refused under all kinds of pretexts. On top of that, refugees from the occupied border areas faced another problem. Those who had no relatives in the capital, or no job or place to study, were not welcome in the already overcrowded city and were sometimes even forcibly removed to the countryside or to Slovakia, where the anti-Jewish feelings were much more prominent than in Bohemia and Moravia.

Picture: Mr. Pollak´s student´s book from Czech Technical University

Despite my situation, I made a last attempt. A remote cousin of mine, actually the daughter of the architect who had invited me to the Paris exhibition was married to a lawyer with good connections in the government. Her new family was rather snobbish, and a person so low as a simple student on the social ladder was not considered worth their attention. Anyway, I turned to her as my last feeble hope. The unexpected happened, her husband intervened somewhere high up and my request for admission at the Czech Technical University was granted. Not only that, but I was given credit for all classes I had attended at the German Technical University, all examinations including the all-important first state examination, were recognized and I could enrol without any academic loss.

My new colleagues there were more or less gracious. My fluency in Czech was at that time rather poor, but I was nonetheless accepted as one of them. That my poor command of the language sometimes led to ludicrous misunderstandings was more helpful than counterproductive. I was assigned to a working group of several students. The name of most I have forgotten, but two are engraved in my memory. One was a Jew from Slovakia. He helped me overcome many of the minor and major obstacles that I, as a newcomer, had to face and we became good friends. The other one played a role in my life after the war, under the communist regime.

A BRUSH WITH THE NUREMBERG ORDINANCE

Nature decree that most young men are attracted to young women, and vice-versa - after all, the continuation of humanity relies upon that law. I was no exception in this regard. However, there were problems. The Nuremberg laws[5] of the Nazi credo made it a capital crime for a Jewish man to have relations with a female of the pure race. I am not sure whether these laws had at that time already been proclaimed in the Protectorate[6], but at any rate their menace was all too present.

---

[5] Two anti-Jewish statutes enacted September 1935 during the Nazi party's national convention in Nuremberg. The first, the Reich Citizenship Law, deprived German Jews of their citizenship and all pertinent, related rights. The second, the Law for the Protection of German Blood and Honor, outlawed marriages of Jews and non-Jews, forbade Jews from employing German females of childbearing age, and prohibited Jews from displaying the German flag. http://motlc.wiesenthal.com/site/pp.asp?c=gvKVLcMVIuG&b=394665

[6] The Nuremberg Laws came into force in the Protectorate on 21 June 1939

In a small place like Příbram, where I came for my student holidays, there were no Jewish girls to go out with; Nor for that matter were there young men. Most public places were already inaccessible to Jews and so I had no choice but to lead, a rather lonely solitary life during my stay. To pass the time I made frequent walks into the surrounding woods, not caring very much where my path led me. Once, on one of these strolls, I came across a small pond in the middle of nowhere. The water looked warm and the scenery calm and peaceful. Nobody seemed to be around and so I decided to take a swim. Unprepared as I was I had to make do without the benefit of swimming trunks. After a short dip, I found that the water was not as warm as it appeared to be. Anyway, I felt fresh and relaxed and climbed back on land to have a nap.

I don't know how long I had been dozing when a noise in the shrubs behind me shook me awake. It appeared that somebody was coming. I had no time to get dressed and just managed to cover the private parts of my body with a shirt, when the source of the noise reached the clearing where I was lying. Imagine my surprise when the newcomer turned out to be a girl, perhaps of my age, in Eve's costume, obviously also with the intention to take a swim. She was no beauty, but well proportioned and endowed. I had not seen a nude woman for perhaps a year and could not pretend that the sight left me unruffled. She appeared to be equally astonished. However, instead of backing into the cover of the shrubs she came close to me and seemed to inspect my body intensely. Then with a sudden movement, she grabbed my shirt and pulled it away. Then she said in German:

"You're Jewish, aren't you? It's the first time I am seeing a Jewish boy this close by. But it does not seem to be too much different from that of out German bulls. Let me see what you have there."

I got more nervous by the minute. It seemed clear that she was German. The region of Příbram was altogether Czech and there were very few Germans living in the area. My surprise visitor likely was a member of the occupation forces, perhaps even of the SS, but there seemed nothing I could do but try to keep cool and my body under control. She may have guessed what was going on in my mind, because all of a sudden she said,

"Don't be afraid, I know that you are Jewish. I have heard that Jews are ideal in lovemaking and I would like to try it with you. I won't tell anybody and I'm sure you won't either."

It was obvious she meant it. I was frightened that she might not have come alone and was just playing treacherous tricks with me. She must have recognized my feelings because she warned me not to even think about resisting her. Well, the idea to resist had certainly crossed my mind. I was very likely stronger than her and also could have tried to run away. But without clothes? What if she would accuse me of having attempted to rape her? A house-to-house search by the Germans would certainly find me. They would believe her story, not mine, and very likely, the outcome would be execution not only of myself, but also of my host and her family. Therefore, I decided to be quiet and submissive and let events take their course.

However, it did not go according to her imagination. My seductress had seemed just about ready to commit the crime of all crimes according to the Nuremberg laws, when my body decided that enough was enough and that was it. My uninvited companion flew into a rage like I had not seen before. She called me all kinds of names and started to beat and kick all over my body. Fortunately, she had no shoes and the kicks were probably hurting her as much as me. After a while when the first rage had evaporated, she went to the place where she had left her clothes declaring that she was to fetch her knife to cut off my testicles.

I am not sure whether she really meant it, but decided that waiting to find out her real intentions would be way too risky. I grabbed my clothes and ran, nude as I was, in the opposite direction from where she had disappeared. I ran as fast as I could until I could not run anymore. Then I stopped, making sure that I did not hear anyone following me. Then I slipped into my clothes and made my way home via a large detour.

It was already dark when I finally reached home and my hosts were already concerned about my absence. I offered them some excuse; like that I had lost my way or something of that kind. I also pretended to have caught a cold and had to stay in bed for a few days. The real reason, of course, was fear that I might meet the lady from the lake again and that she might recognize me. Of course, I could not stay at home forever. When after a few days I finally ventured out into the street again, I carefully looked around scrutinizing the faces of all the young women I met. Fortunately, none of them were the one I was looking for and luckily, I never saw her again.

THE ONSET OF THE "FINAL SOLUTION"

MY APPRENTICESHIP

I was a student again, but not for long. Everything had ended and begun on 17 November 1939.

The occupation of the western part of the former Czechoslovakia, now the Protectorate of Bohemia and Moravia, had already been well established, but little did we guess at that time all its consequences. That Jewish students had been expelled from the German universities was taken as an inconvenience and we were happy that nothing of that kind, had as yet, happened at the Czech schools.

I was a student of electrical engineering at that time. I woke up late that day and was in a hurry to attend my first lecture at 10 a.m. I jumped out of the tram and rushed to the main entrance. Whether something was unusual there I did not notice; I was in too much of a hurry. Only a few steps into the dark entrance corridor I stumbled over something, and would have fallen if somebody would not have caught me in his arms. A quick glance showed somebody was wearing a German uniform and the gadget over which I had stumbled was the tripod of a heavy machine gun, its muzzle pointing towards the gate. I do not remember whether I muttered an apology or thank you. Only that I ran away as fast as I could and jumped into a tram just leaving the stop, not even looking at its number. I made it home safe and sound.

Listening to the radio, I learned that all institutions of higher learning, including universities, were closed from that day forward and that students had to look for useful jobs or face the danger of being drafted to the labour organization named after its founder and leader, Fritz Todt, a prominent Nazi. The latter alternative did not sound too attractive, especially not for somebody of the inferior race. What should I do?

Because German young men had been drafted into the army, labour, and especially skilled labour, was a scarce commodity. Finding a job was very difficult for any former student, but for a student with the big red letter J (for Jew) on his identity card, it was absolutely impossible. And that message was brought home ever more forcefully after each of many fruitless presentations.

"We would very much like to hire you, but..." was the stereotypical refrain. On the other hand, giving up the search seemed to be an open invitation to the Gestapo and similar "humane" institutions. After a couple of weeks of fruitless search, a non-Jewish friend recommended that I should present myself at the "Private Phone Company" in downtown Prague. It appeared to be a crazy idea, but perhaps that's why it seemed appropriate at that crazy time. I knew the company; it was a branch plant of a much bigger German company, which until recently had been Jewish-owned and only a few months ago had been "Aryanised". The Jewish owner had made his escape in time and the new Aryan manager was a German, Mr. Engling, the former chief engineer of the firm. He was considered a decent, honest person who wore the swastika on his lapel only because he had to. He had been in friendly relations with the former Jewish owner and there were rumours that these relations were not entirely abandoned.

I had made up my mind and visited him one morning in December, armed with a verbal recommendation of the former owner who had been a vague acquaintance of mine. I really did not expect very much, but I had to try. When I came and explained my request to the secretary, still one of the former personnel, she just shook her head but ushered me in to see the new boss. He was sitting at the desk of the former owner with a big swastika pin in his lapel. The only other change in the room was a big portrait of the great Führer, which decorated the wall behind him.

"What do you want?" he said in not too friendly a manner. I explained that I was a student of electrical engineering that the University was closed and I was looking for a job. He listened silently to my brief presentation and remained in silence long after I had finished. Finally he said:

"Are you aware of what you are asking for? Are you aware of the risk I am incurring by giving you a job? Yes, I understand, you must avoid being drafted into the Todt Organization."

"Yes sir, that is one of the reasons."

"In which year were you?"

"The third."

"Do you know something about telephones?"

"Not much, but I will learn, if you give me the opportunity."

"You have courage. Do you have some money to live on?"

"Not too much but I am modest."

He looked me up and down, obviously reflecting but not saying a word. Finally, he said, "I cannot give you a reply right away. Come back in a week's time and I'll see whether I can do something for you. But now you had better go."

These words were actually much more than the outright refusal I had half expected and a glimmer of hope took hold in my mind.

I came back a week later to the minute. This time I was received by the secretary. Her first words sounded desperate. "Mr. Engling regrets that given the political situation he cannot accept you as an engineer or even a technician." She paused and I was about to say a few words that I understood and wanted to leave. Before I summoned the courage, she continued:

"We need personnel for our repair and maintenance department. Of course, you don't have the practical skills and experience for that. You can acquire them in our workshop as an apprentice. Are you prepared to accept that position? If you are, you can start next Monday."

It was a question, but both she and the manager knew very well that I was in no position to refuse or bargain. It was obvious that as an apprentice I would have no ordinary salary, only a few crowns as pocket money.

Next Monday morning I showed up at the company and was assigned a seat at the main bench in the workshop. A Mr. K. became my supervisor and instructor. I soon found out that he was an enthusiastic friend of the Soviet Union, finding everything Stalin did great and justifiable. He tried to convert me to his credo and when he did not succeed to his liking, he lost all interest in me. He did not forget that when he became a big shot after the communist takeover in 1948. Although he refused to be of any assistance to me, he was not overtly against me, either. Whether Mr. Engling knew about his Stalinist sentiments, I do not know.

It was a tough time, and not only financially. My co-workers did not appreciate having a former student and were jealous of my engineering background. From my university classes, I had a reasonable amount of theoretical knowledge about telephone technology and now I learned the practical skills a maintenance person in that field had to master. This combination gave me a big advantage over my workmates and I was called to any complicated job. Later, when I was an inmate of the Theresienstadt ghetto, this rare combination of manual skills and theoretical knowledge helped save my life.

I have to say that Mr. Engling helped where he could, not only me but other victims of the Nazi regime as well, and he saved many Jewish and Czech lives, mine included. I will return to this man in an episode where he saved my life and that of the "Arbeitskommando" to which I was attached.

In spite of all that, he met a terrible and thoroughly undeserved end. In the last days of the war, before the German capitulation, at the time of the Prague uprising in May 1945, he made the mistake of not fleeing in time and was hanged by a lynch mob from a lantern stand in one of the suburbs of Prague.

My apprenticeship lasted about eight months, until a general decree of the Reichsprotektor Heydrich ordered all Jews working in a non-Jewish enterprise, at that time virtually all Jews, had to be dismissed..

Gradually, we became adjusted to the tightening of the restrictions upon Jewish life. And with their acceptance as a part of Jewish life in wartime Germany, life passed on almost with a degree of normalcy. My family was by no means rich, but we lived in a kind of barter economy where my uncle's patients paid for his services in kind, mostly with agricultural and cattlemen's products. So food was never a problem.

Now the cost of food was the biggest drain on my financial resources, forcing a strict dietary economy upon me. Some food products were becoming scarce or limited and purchases on the black market were without question compounded by the danger of being caught in the act.

FATHER'S WATCH

My uncle in Postoloprty had rented a safety box at a large bank, formerly German-Jewish, in the centre of Prague. He had deposited there the jewellery of my mother and the little I had inherited from my father. I do not remember whether somebody had warned me or whether I became suspicious by myself, that a safety deposit box owned by a Jew would be an open invitation for the Gestapo, but anyway, the next day I went to the bank with the intent of emptying the box. Alas, it was too late. The Gestapo had been there before me.

When I came to the bank, I was very politely asked to sign a declaration, that I was non-Jewish. When I refused to do that, they told me that the safety deposit box was opened and that I could choose one item to my liking to take with me. The remainder would likely be forfeited in favour of the Reich. I chose a golden watch that had belonged to my father.

To this day, I do not know whether the bank official who permitted me to take home father's watch did so on his own as a favour to me or whether he had instructions in this regard. Anyway, the remaining contents of the box were inventoried, I had to sign the list of contents and the officials co-signed it. The box was sealed and put back into its old place in the strong room. That was the end of it and I left.

During the time of my internment, it was hidden with my non-Jewish friend who returned it to me after the war. It is still in my possession, probably the only piece of value that survived the war intact. I have no photos of my father or of my uncle and aunt, and only a small picture of my mother that was hidden in a pendant and attached to that watch.

After the war, I enquired at the bank and was shown a paper with an illegible signature and the stamp of some high-level German office; I do not remember which one. The text said that my safety deposit box was to be unsealed and its contents issued to the bearer of that paper. The paper was dated on one of the last days before the German surrender.

Years later, I had the opportunity to claim restitution of the contents of that safety box, particularly of my mother's jewellery, from some office in Berlin. The claim was rejected. I had not put too much confidence into my claim and, therefore, the rejection per se did not affect me too much. However, what did touch me was that the rejection was based upon the testimony of a Mr. P, the son of my shorthand teacher in Postoloprty. I do not know what office Mr. P had held during the occupation, but his claim was that officials of the Czech puppet government emptied the safety deposit box and that the German authorities had nothing to do with it. However ludicrous that statement, the West German authorities gave it credence and there was nothing I could do about it.

MY FRIEND BELA

AT STUDIES

When I arrived at the Czech Technical University, I found myself in a totally new environment. Everything was unfamiliar and my poor knowledge of the language did not make things easier for me. So I was more than happy when two students in the same class as me offered to help and in a short time we became good friends. Only much later I found out that both were members of the communist underground and had for one reason or another been instructed by the party to help me. After the war and after the communist coup in 1948, one of them became a high-ranking member of the party and government bureaucracy. Our old friendship from the times of the protectorate was forgotten by then. Though I did not think he tried to harm me, he was not prepared to lift a finger when I had fallen victim to one of the frequent political purges. I do not know where he lives but I presume he is still alive and so I will not mention his name. He plays no role in any other episode.

Much closer were my relations with the other one, Bela. He is still alive, living in South America. I was in the city where he is living and tried to phone him, but I did not succeed in reaching him and he never returned my call. So, I assume our old friendship is also gone, but that will not prevent me from talking about him during those by-gone times.

Bela came from a poor Jewish family living in Slovakia, then the eastern part of Czechoslovakia. One of the first things Hitler did after the invasion of the Western parts of that country, Bohemia and Moravia, was to make Slovakia an "independent" country and his ally. The government of that time followed an ideology that was a strange mixture of fascist ideas and religious concepts. It was quite pliable to Hitler's wishes. Hitler's reward was to leave the country formally independent and to consider it as Germany's friend.

Anti-Jewish measures were adopted, but they were, especially in the early days, much milder that those in the Protectorate, which was under direct occupation. As a citizen of Slovakia, Bela was exempt from the discriminatory measures against the Jews of the Protectorate. He was not obliged to wear the yellow Star of David on his chest and his identity papers were not stamped with the big red J for Jewish. The curfew regulations forbidding Jews to leave their homes after eight o'clock did not apply to him either.

At the time we met, Bela led a life the same as any other non-Jewish citizen of the capital. We continued to be friends even after the closure of all Czech colleges and universities in November 1939. Many times he prodded me to follow his example, to dispose of the yellow star all Jews in the Protectorate, without exception, had to wear from October 1, 1941, and to enjoy life freely in his company. For better or worse, I was too cautious to follow his bidding. In Prague, he was living in a villa belonging to the wealthy parents of a fellow student, not far from the place where I was living. He and his host's son were good friends. At that time, I did not know that both were enthusiastic members of the communist underground.

The two boys were operating a radio transmitter broadcasting news and communist propaganda. Whether they did that on their own or upon instruction from the underground, I cannot say. Anyway, they did it in an amateurish way, with minimum precautions against discovery and detection. In spite of that, they felt safe that their system was eluding the efforts of the Gestapo to locate it. Unfortunately, they were wrong. The roaming surveillance cars of the Gestapo did not have much trouble monitoring their transmissions and pinpointing the place where they originated. For a long time nothing happened, although the two were almost certainly kept under observation. Whether the reason was the pact of "Friendship" with Stalin, or just the hope of catching a larger group of members of a clandestine network, is hard to tell. Nor am I sure when they finally decided to strike. Perhaps it was the assassination of the SS general Heidrich, then the top official of the German administration, the "Reichsprotector" and the chief of the security services, Sicherheitsdienst. Or it may have been the anticipation of the invasion of the Soviet Union and of the breakdown of the pact with Stalin. Whatever the reason, when they finally decided to strike, they did it unexpectedly and with deadly precision.

When it happened, I was already an inmate, an anonymous number in the Terezín concentration camp. I learned details of the event only after the war.

One exciting and scary episode from the early days of our friendship, still vivid in my mind, illustrates his attitude and style.

Bela had many girlfriends, all of them non-Jewish. He would have been prepared to share his conquests with me, if I had not been too timid for that. One of these girls was an extremely pretty young woman perhaps our age or maybe somewhat younger. She dreamt of getting married and in order to earn some money for her dowry she worked as a high-class call girl for members of the Prague high society. One of her regular customers was a prominent minister of the last government of independent Czechoslovakia. Mr. Kovacz (not his real name) was an elderly gentleman of the old school, but still fond of young women. He was an ardent admirer of the physical beauty and attractiveness of this girl, and was prepared to pay well for the enjoyment she was able to offer. Unfortunately, his sexual potency had all but disappeared with age. So in order to enjoy their rendezvous, the two had to use all kinds of special methods. Our friend's professional expertise had given her the requisite skills to satisfy his most exotic demands. She was more than ready to test these skills on the two of us and seemed to enjoy the reaction of our young bodies. Though I do not know for sure, I presume this enjoyment was her only reward. Encounters of that kind were quite frequent. For one reason or another, Bela seemed to savour my presence and reactions.

One afternoon, I believe it was in March 1940, the threesome of ours was again involved in these activities at Bela's apartment. We had been at it already quite some time, when all of a sudden the doorbell rang. Bela did not expect any visitors and the sound of the bell acted like a cold shower, rapidly cooling our overheated anticipations. The precariousness of our situation came suddenly to my awareness. In case somebody had snitched on us, the person in most danger would be me. Whether Bela's Slovak passport would be sufficient to keep him out of harm's way was at least questionable and that the girl would be in trouble, as well, was virtually certain. At that moment, Bela did not lose his composure. He ordered the girl and me into the washroom, where we stood squeezed together waiting for things to come.

Bela donned a housecoat and went to answer the door. Outside was a Czech policeman, obviously quite embarrassed. He asked my friend whether he was the only one in the apartment. When answered in the affirmative, he demanded to see Bela's I.D. His Slovak passport saved the day. The policeman glanced at it just perfunctorily and excused himself, saying that he had been told to investigate whether one of these damned Jews was not living there clandestinely. He apologized once more and left.

When he was gone, we came out of our hiding place, but the interest in continuing our erotic games was gone. The girl dressed, and after having made certain that the house was not under observation, she left. A few minutes later, it was my turn to slip out and to return to my nearby home. It was the last time we dared engage in games of that kind and also the last time that I visited Bela's home. We both had a shock and interpreted the policeman's visit as a warning not to be disregarded.

Though I took that warning very seriously, Bela was less concerned. He believed that it was my presence, which had triggered the policeman's call, and felt that if I would not show up at his place again, everything would return to normal. He and his landlord's son continued their political broadcasting (I did not know at that time that the two were operating a secret radio transmitter), as if nothing had happened. The consequences became evident only much later and they were catastrophic. I learned about them only after the war when I had returned to Prague and met Bela and other former students. Our friendship was renewed when we met again, each of us having gone through battles of different kinds to survive. What the wartime experiences of both of us had in common was a life fraught with mortal dangers, dangers that could crop up any day.

BELA'S WARTIME ADVENTURES

The events in this chapter come largely from Bela's own account. They were checked, though, against what I heard from others, principally Bela's (and my) former friend, who had become his main enemy. Some parts were incoherent, and some were not told at all, under the pretext of being military secrets. I had to piece these things painstakingly together, but I believe they are accurate.

I have already mentioned that Bela and the son of his landlord were operating a clandestine radio transmitter. Maybe they had some contacts with the KGB[7] and/or the intelligence agency of one of the Western powers and their broadcasts were intended for them. Unfortunately, neither their technical equipment nor the way they operated was a match for the sophisticated surveillance devices of the Gestapo. The transmitter they operated was probably located in no time. Surveillance was still easier, because the boys were using open language and their unsophisticated facility enabled detecting the time routine. Perhaps the news they were offering was of little value and the boys were considered expendable. Perhaps they were even regarded as sacrificial offerings. I don't know. Anyway, what had to happen, happened. The Gestapo knew about their station apparently a long time without openly intervening. Perhaps they were aware that they were dealing with amateurs and were waiting in the hope to catch bigger fish. Then they struck.

On that day, Bela had been on a cycling excursion in the environs of Prague. As luck would had it he was returning to his residence late in the evening. Near his place, his girlfriend of the time was waiting for him, telling him not to return to his house, that the Gestapo were there waiting for him, and that they had arrested his friend and all his family. That was indeed the case. Though nobody seemed to know their immediate fate at the hands of the Gestapo, the fact is that none of them returned after the war.

Bela obeyed the warning and spent the night somewhere in the woods near Prague. He was then given forged papers by the underground and smuggled into a transport of workers to Germany. His almost complete engineering education was helpful and in a relatively short time, he became foreman of a test station for aircraft engines in the former Austria. Here he obviously established new links to various intelligence organizations not only of the Russians but also of the Western allies. That activity was discovered in late 1944. Again, he was warned in time and managed to escape for a

---

7 Officially, KGB emerged in 1954. It may have been one of its predecessors, NKVD or NKGB, doing the same.

second time the waiting net of the Gestapo. He did so with the help of the newer more courageous and active Czech underground or perhaps also the vast forests straddling the border between Bohemia and Bavaria. Here he succeeded in surviving the winter and spring of 1945.

With the advancing American army and with the Russian troops, he returned in May 1945 to Prague, and was given a hero's welcome. He had plenty of medals and letters of distinction from both the Red army and the Western intelligence services. I do not know the details of his activity during the years in Vienna that earned him all these honours. He never bragged about it and when talk turned to that subject, he clammed up immediately.

When I returned from the Konzentrationslager, my first concern was obviously to finish my studies and to obtain my degree. That's where I met Bela again. Our friendship seemingly had not suffered from the years of separation and the different experiences we had gone through. Without going into factual details and never mentioning names, even if they were certain to be code names, he told me titbits about his life in Austria, and about his efforts to pass on details about improvements and innovations on the aircraft engines he had to test, many of them experimental designs. He told me about long sleepless nights and his fear at any unusual noise near his lodging, which might be caused by the Gestapo fiends about to fetch him. I, in turn, told him about life in Terezín and similar sleepless nights in expectation of summons to a transport.

Bela had been assigned an apartment in downtown Prague in a prime location. For me, that apartment had a strange history tied to it.

In the pre-Hitler period, it had belonged to a good friend of ours, a Jew like us. He had been a victim of the Gestapo's revenge for the assassination of their supreme chief Reinhard Heydrich in 1942, by a commando unit sent by the Czechoslovak government in exile. He never returned. The vacated apartment had been given to Mr. P, already mentioned in connection with the safety box and family jewels. I remember him well because he was a fanatic Nazi already in Postoloprty. He hated me for reasons I did not quite understand. I am good friends with most of the former German population of Postoloprty who were expelled after the war and live mostly in Germany now. Not with him, though; he has kept his hatred to this day. Unfortunately, circumstances allowed him to demonstrate this hatred even many years after the war. Mr. P. had to flee Prague after the war and it was his apartment which, fully equipped, was given to Bela.

We both had little confidence in our future in Czechoslovakia and were making all kinds of plans to emigrate. Late in 1947, Bela came to me saying that he had made up his mind and was going to apply soon for a visa to a South America country; I believe it was Chile. He invited me to join him. I agreed and we applied jointly the following week, but whilst he was given the visa almost immediately, I was turned down. In retrospect, I believe that he was warned of the coming communist coup d'état and that his visa application was probably supported by one of the Western intelligence agencies with whom he had cooperated during the war.

That hypothesis was supported by the fact that after the 1948 "February Revolution", a communist putsch in Czechoslovakia, I was repeatedly interrogated by the communist secret police who wanted to know Bela's whereabouts, which I of course, pretended not to know. Probably to turn me against him, they told me all kinds of stories about Bela's treacherous behaviour during the war and his clandestine cooperation with the Gestapo, which had supposedly cost the lives of many comrades. I did not put much faith into the truth of these allegations but was equally at a loss about their reasons. Maybe because he cooperated during the war not exclusively with the Soviet, but also with Western intelligence agencies and the intent was to punish him for that. Whatever the reason, I am certain he was apprehensive enough not to put his faith into a future Stalinist regime.

After he left, I got a few letters from different places in South America. Though these letters and cards did not tell too much, they gave the appearance that his departure (or perhaps flight) was rather adventurous. The letters reinforced the impression that a powerful organization held its protective hand over him and sheltered him from many mishaps. I have seen him since then only once, during a brief visit to his residence in South America. At later visits, he declined to see me.

BEFORE THE HELL GATES OPENED

MY LAST CHANCE

It was well after my forced move to the small quarters at the periphery of Prague under the watchful eyes of my landlady "the dragon" when, quite unexpectedly, I got an offer to apply for admission and a scholarship at a university in the United States, I believe in South Carolina. I do not know who had arranged for that, although I believe it was the Joint.[8] Naturally, I signed the papers on the spot and returned them to the address shown. For several months I did not get a reply; it was as if the papers had never arrived. The return address given was in a suburb of Prague, quite far from my place. You had to cross the Vltava River to get there.

At that time, you went as a Jew to the downtown area only in an urgent case. Downtown teemed with Germans in uniform and in plain clothes and though there was no express prohibition to enter downtown, one tried to avoid it if possible. Despite that, I one day tried to discover with what kind of organization I had been in touch. I took the train to that suburb and arrived there without incident. It took some effort to find the street and house number where I had been instructed to send my papers. What I found was a large and fairly shabby apartment house with no outward sign that it might be the seat of an organization or an office. I went in and examined the list of tenants at the door, but none of the names sounded familiar. I could not even ask, not knowing for whom I should ask. I went home without success and that was the end of my last chance.

---

[8] The American Jewish Joint Distribution Committee, Inc.

GOOD-HEARTED GESTAPO GUY

Before the Protectorate had been established,[9] mail between the Sudeten and Prague was almost normal and I received letters from my uncle and aunt fairly regularly. Then there was an interruption of several months. I had no means of finding out why and to say that I was concerned would definitely be an understatement. Finally, the long-awaited letter arrived. I looked at the postmark only to find out that instead of the familiar Postoloprty, it was marked Edersgrün, a name I had never heard before. I tore the envelope open and devoured its contents.

In brief, my uncle wrote that my auntie had died whilst they were still in Postoloprty and was not buried in the Jewish cemetery of Postoloprty, but in a new cemetery in Michelup (Měcholupy), a village near my high school city of Žatec. That he had been deported to an intermediate camp for Jews in Edersgrün (Odeř) near Karlovy Vary, and that he was reasonably well. Also, that our house in Postoloprty had been given to a police officer from Upper Silesia, and he shared the cell in that camp with Mr. Kepl, a Jewish farmer, also from Postoloprty. The latter sentence and its wording assumed in the following days an importance of its own. Of course, all correspondence to and from a camp was censored and the censor decided whether some section of the letter should be blackened out or whether the whole letter should be destroyed.

A few days later, I got a letter from the Gestapo headquarters to report on that day to the Petchek Palace, the main office of the Gestapo in Prague. Perhaps I do not have to emphasize that such a summons did not contribute to my peace of mind. Rumours abounded about (mainly Jewish) people who had received such an invitation and were never seen again. But ignoring the summons did not seem a practical response either. A person caught after such a "crime" was certain to face the benevolent attention of the Gestapo.

I collected all the courage I could muster and marched, on the day and hour specified in the letter, into the lion's den. Of course, I had not the slightest idea what the whole matter was about. I showed my citation at the entrance and a uniformed guard guided me several floors up where I was

[9] 16 March 1939

asked to wait in the corridor until the officer in charge of my case would summon me. I had to wait for an hour or so until he arrived. He beckoned me into his office and let me sit down, whilst he took out his pistol and emptied its magazine. Then he opened the drawer, took out a paper and studied it. The paper looked like a photocopy of my uncle's letter.

The interrogation started with questions, which sounded quite innocent. This lasted quite a while before turning to the main subject, the apparent reason for why I had been summoned.

"Your uncle is a communist?" he barked suddenly.

"Certainly not, nor has he ever been", was my reply.

"And why does he write that he is in the same cell as that other fellow who we know is a communist? And aren't you a communist as well?"

Now, being in the hands of the Gestapo as a Jew was bad, but to be branded as a Jew and a communist amounted to a death sentence. The seriousness of my situation became all of a sudden quite clear to me and I was grasping for the right answer. To make a long story short, my reply was:

"My uncle is obviously a prisoner sharing his cell with that other person. Neither he nor I have ever been politically active, let alone communists." The Gestapo man then leafed through his papers, apparently looking at inmates from Edersgrün, and mumbled something like,

"Those idiots!"

Turning to me he said, "For today, you can go. Next month a ship will be leaving from Pressburg[10] to Israel. Pack your things and go there as fast as you can. I'll show you what may be in store for you, if you don't listen. Come with me!"

We took the elevator down several floors to the vast underground of the building and he opened one door. In the dimly lit room there was a low table covered with leather or plastic. A man was strapped to that table with his belly down. I could not see it clearly, but his mouth seemed to be covered by some material, apparently to prevent him from crying out. His pants and underwear had been removed and his buttocks were red and bleeding, and a man in uniform was busy rubbing some white material into the wounds. "It is salt and it hurts", the Gestapo man guiding me remarked casually.

---

[10] Bratislava, the capital of Slovakia

He then slammed the door of the chamber shut and brought me to the entrance, where he released me. I spent the following night with little sleep, pondering what to do. I did not go to Pressburg and stayed in Prague until my later deportation.

REPRESSIONS ESCALATE

The occupation of the country was followed by a period of relative calm, but that did not last long. After perhaps half a year or so, Hitler made it abundantly clear that his territorial aspirations were far from satisfied. This time his arm was pointed east, at Poland. That was the spark that ignited the war, which soon was to engulf much of the world.

In the meantime, the screws of oppression against the Jews were tightened. I do not remember the exact chronological order and, therefore, am asking the reader's forgiveness for any mistake in the sequence of events.

Our freedom to move even within the city limits was severely limited. Prague did not have a subway at that time, just trams, and buses were few and far between. The city at that time was already widely spread out, and distances were mostly too large to be covered on foot. Private cars were a rarity and I doubt that a Jew, even if he could afford it, would have been able to obtain a driver's license. Rather, I believe the car would have been confiscated. The main means of public transport were electric trams. Jews were allowed to use only the last car. If there was only a single car, tough luck. Nor were they allowed to be in the streets after eight o'clock in the evening. In addition, most restaurants and many shops sported a sign in large letters; "Jews undesirable", or something similar.

Two episodes that related to the curfew are stuck in my memory. It was in the centre of Prague, on the Wenceslas Square at the time when we already had to wear the yellow Star of David with the bold inscription "Jew" plainly visible on the outer garment. I was walking up the hill when I was approached by a German soldier in uniform. Now, a Jew being approached by a German in uniform was bound to trigger some cold shivers down the spine. But there was no chance to evade that encounter. You can imagine my surprise when the soldier addressed me by my first name, asking me in a friendly way, how I was doing. Then I recognized him. He was the son of a tailor in Postoloprty, a family half Czech, half German. They were one of the few mixed families who chose to stay when the town was annexed by the Germans. Now he regretted that, but it was too late. I warned him that it might be dangerous for him to be seen in the street conversing with a Jew. He did not listen, though, complaining bitterly about his life since the occupation. It took about an hour, walking up and down the square. I was nervous more for his sake than for mine. Finally, we parted, and I never saw him again.

WELCOME TO THERESIENSTADT

FROM FORTRESS TO GAOL TO GHETTO

Terezín is a fortress town built at the end of the 18th century by the Austrian Emperor Josef II to defend the route from Dresden to Prague, the capital of Bohemia, against possible invasions by the Prussian army. He had named it Theresienstadt, after his mother, Empress Marie Theresa. In its time, it represented the zenith of bastion fortification building in Europe, but it never served that purpose. It was maintained as a military stronghold and garrison town until the 1880s, and after that its buildings were used as a state prison.

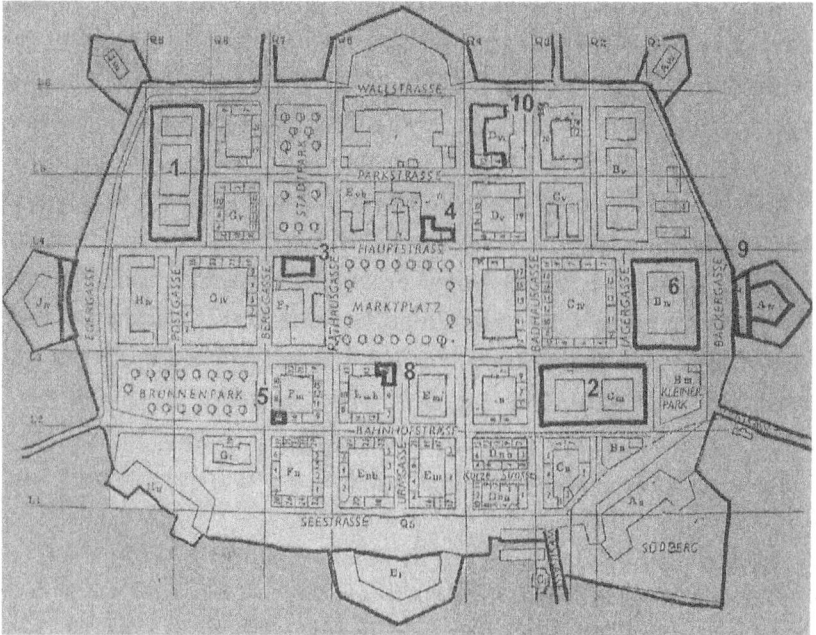

Picture: Old map of both fortresses.

Militarily, the old fortress was of little or no value against modern weaponry. However, the high wall surrounding the town and the deep escarpment with only few possible exit gates made it an easily guarded prison. Besides the barracks, the garrison town (called the Main Fortress), included many civilian apartment houses. When the Germans decided to convert it to a Jewish ghetto, the Czech civilian population was forced to leave. Terezín became a concentration camp for that "racial scum", whose extermination Hitler considered his God-given duty. It served, in essence, as a transit point for transports to other camps where the actual "final solution of the Jewish problem" was to be carried out.

The main ghetto had been established in the Main Fortress. The perimeter was guarded by Czech gendarmes who, of course, took their orders from the SS command of the camp. The same applied to the Jewish Council of Elders, which was in charge of internal administration of the camp but had to follow the orders of the SS command and implement them.

A kilometre east of the ghetto camp, across the Ohře River, is the Small Fortress. Its original purpose had been the defence of the access roads to the Main Fortress. In June 1940, Prague Gestapo command took it over and established a police prison, and inmates immediately began construction of prison barracks.

As the name implies, it is much smaller than the Main Fortress, but Gestapo could not ignore the fort with its high walls and surrounding water-filled trenches, and established a second "general purpose" concentration camp. The term "general purpose" means that the camp was not intended solely for inmates from a specific segment of the population. Though not an "extermination camp" in the strict sense as Auschwitz and others, it was feared by potential inmates as one of the cruellest camps of all. Few "yellow stars" who were sent to the Small Fortress from the ghetto managed to survive the offered hospitality there for any length of time.

Illustration: The post stamp and banknotes of the Theresienstadt ghetto, components of the disguise of this KZ as a showpiece internment facility.

Photo: An ordinary ghetto street. (Photo archive of the Jewish Museum in Prague)

THERESIENSTADT - THE SHOWCASE KZ

The Germans assigned the ghetto of Theresienstadt a twin mission. First, it was to serve as a transit camp for Jewish deportees from the Protectorate before they could be shipped to the extermination camps in the east, mainly in Poland. Second, it was to be used as a "show internment" facility to demonstrate to the outside world that the Jews were treated in a relatively humane way and not in a barbaric fashion, as "Grevelpropaganda (horror propaganda) wanted the world to believe." The reality was much worse than anything labelled as "horror propaganda" and became known only much later. It was so bad, so terrible, that the younger generation of today finds it hard to believe.

Probably not from its inception but soon afterwards Theresienstadt was intended as a sort of Potemkin's villages for foreign visitors such as the Red Cross delegations, politicians and journalists. The intent was to refute the rumours of the inhumanity of the concentration camps and the mass murder of Jews and other "sub humans", which leaked out of the walled fortress from time to time despite all efforts of the SS, and were smuggled to the West.

The designation of Theresienstadt as a showcase of the German system of concentration camps was the reason that it was spared the worst atrocities. These took place in the other camps to which 97% of the more than 300,000 Jews first sent to Theresienstadt were deported. There were plenty of other concentration camps where those methods of treatment could be carried out and were much more hidden from the eyes of the world.

In keeping with the camp's intention, the SS were forbidden to carry out public tortures and executions. This is not to say that physical or psychological torture did not exist, but when it occurred, it was mostly the work of individual members of the SS guard and was carefully kept under wraps. To prevent victims from talking, they were inevitably shipped off on the next transport where they were silenced forever.

The appearance of a benign internment camp was occasionally boosted by special measures. This occurred mainly when a foreign delegate, for example, of the Red Cross was expected. Buildings were repainted and food became, for the time of the visit, ample and even tasty. In one such

"Verschönerungsaktion" (improvement action), children were given tins of sardines and had to say to the camp commander, (who pretended to play with them), "Oh, no, Uncle Rahm, again sardines!"

Of course, when all foreign visitors to be duped were gone, the prisoners' life in the ghetto changed dramatically. The tins had to be returned unopened, and were carefully counted. Another part of the scheme was the issuance of ghetto money and so-called "shops" where some merchandise could be bought. Naturally, the assortment available was extremely limited even when visitors were around. When they left, mustard and relish-like preparations were the only things available. The possession of real money was, of course, prohibited. The same applied to cigarettes, which together with bread (military style loaves) were the internal currency of the ghetto. Smoking was not allowed and smokers caught by the SS found themselves in the next "resettlement" transport to the east. Those transported could call themselves "lucky" that in the transport list behind their name and original transport number were not added the innocent-looking letters RU (Rückkehr unerwünscht - return undesirable).

There was also a special squad of women we called "lady birds" (berušky in Czech, a play on words; "berušky" - those who take away - "confiscators") who searched the suitcases or boxes where the few personal belongings a person could own in the ghetto were stored, whilst the owners were at work. Their official mission was to search for cigarettes and other prohibited contraband but did not disdain other things they fancied. I do not smoke, but I used to enjoy the taste of tobacco. In the ghetto I did light up occasionally and only when it appeared reasonably safe to do so. I did so as an act of defiance to the Germans and perhaps as a demonstration of macho courage.

A "coffee shop" also existed where you could sit when not at work for an hour or so, and for ghetto money sip a cup of Ersatzkaffee (coffee substitute). There was also a musical band and an organised group of painters. For children and youngsters, a kinderheim (day care home) existed, where children were under the care of young girls, whilst their mothers were working. All these establishments were intended for the benefit of visitors from the outside world and had little or no effect upon the life of the vast majority of the camp's population.

SNAPSHOTS OF LIFE INSIDE THE WALLS

The events narrated on the following pages occurred in the Main Fortress. They are based throughout upon personal experience and I vouch for their truthfulness. An exception is the few episodes, which are based upon second hand information. The sources for these episodes I consider reliable, though the indirect transmission involved may have coloured some the details.

THE STORY OF LOST LUGGAGE

Never argue with fate. What appears as a disaster today may become a blessing tomorrow. The following story may serve as an example for that age-old wisdom.

I have already mentioned that in the fall of 1941 a decree of the Reichsprotektor ordered all Jews still employed to be fired. I was of course no exception. At about the same time, deportations began, first to a ghetto in Litzmannstadt, the name the Nazis had given to the Polish city of Lodź. Soon rumours started to circulate in Prague that a new ghetto was to be opened in the old fortress of Terezín, and it did not take long until the first two advance transports, named AK (Aufbaukommando), were dispatched there. Young men predominantly formed those transports. They were to construct the physical facilities necessary for the operation of the ghetto, which was to hold, at times, around fifty thousand prisoners. The deadline given to the boys of the AK was more than tight. As an enticement, they were promised a degree of preferential treatment and protection from deportation east. For a limited time, the promise was kept but later broken, as so many other promises made by the "Übermenschen" (supermen)" from the master race.

As the construction work progressed, the civilian population of the walled town was evacuated. The military barracks had already been evacuated, and the transports began to roll. Finally, in February 1942, it became my turn. I packed the few belongings the deportees were allowed to take and confided them to the luggage service organized by the Jewish community of Prague. Its purpose was not so much to assist the deportees but to make the process less conspicuous and also to facilitate their loading into the prepared cattle car at the railway station. When the luggage was gone, I fell into desperation. My adoptive father had been a country doctor and I had salvaged, just in case, some tablets of morphine. I had enough to extinguish forever all pains a person might suffer. That might have been the end of the story.

Fate had decided otherwise, though. Unplanned, unexpected, my girlfriend decided to drop by. She had a key and when nobody answered the door, she entered and found me unconscious on the floor. An emergency call to the Jewish hospital produced an ambulance car, which brought me to the hospital where after two days' fight with the insidious drug I was brought back to life. I still remember that when I came out of the coma I had the impression that I was in a different world with the physicians and nurses in their white gowns floating around me like ghosts. Well, the summons to the camp was waiting and, after a few days of recovery, I was judged fit for deportation and on a stretcher carried into the waiting special train.

When I arrived at the camp, I happened to find an old friend of mine, who was working in the kitchen. He supplied me clandestinely with some more food and I recovered fairly quickly. I was still listed as sick and therefore not assigned to any work, and I was not in any hurry to volunteer. A grave mistake, as soon was to become evident.

Two weeks went by rather uneventfully, a deceptive calm, which soon turned over into excitement and fear. A new transport to the East was announced. Later, much later, I learned that it was destined for the infamous death camp Treblinka and it was doubtful that few, if any, of the participants would survive the war.

To make the deception complete and to calm any fears, it was announced that the new transport was to be a second "Aufbaukommando" for a camp similar to that in Theresienstadt, but far in eastern Poland, which would serve as a permanent settlement for the Jewish population. One thousand persons should go there. Due to its purpose, most of the participants were to be young single men, without any occupation important for the operation of the present camp. All persons in that category should get ready. A final list of the selected names was to be distributed during the night and boarding was to begin in the early morning hours.

The definition of persons to be primarily selected seemed to be tailor-made and I had little doubt that my name would appear on the list. Name is perhaps the wrong word as in most cases, it was not the name but the transport number that was used for identification. In my case, the number was X715 and I don't think I will ever forget it. X designating the original transport[11] and 715 the serial number of that transport. At that time, we did not know about gas chambers and similar approaches to the final solution favoured by the Nazis. The destination of the transport was secret and even if it had been known, few could have associated any definite meaning to the word Treblinka. Even in such case, you prefer the devil you know to the one you don't.

Regardless of my wishes, it seemed fairly certain that I would be selected and there was little I could do to avert it. Therefore, it was better to be prepared. Eastern Poland was supposed to be cold in winter, much colder than Terezín and an abundance of heating material was the least one would expect. To make it worse, my luggage had not yet arrived and was presumably left in Prague. I had very few warm things, besides what I had been wearing when I was brought to the hospital and a few spare things my girlfriend had brought later.

With this dismal outlook in mind, I went to the Jewish administrator of the barracks which were now my home, and presented him with my predicament. He was compassionate, and it may be that he knew more than I, and explained that in the barracks of the main administration they had a small supply of the things I was missing and, given the circumstances, they might give me something. He asked a ghetto policeman (yes, the ghetto had its own police, Ghettowache) to take me to those barracks and then back. At night the streets of the ghetto were, of course, off limits for all except those who had a special permit. The central administration was located in the Magdeburg barracks, a quarter of an hour from the barracks where I was accommodated.

All lights were on in testimony of the hectic activity inside. The guard

---

[11] The transport list X of 12 February 1942 contains the names of 1,000 persons deported for racial reasons from Prague to Terezín.

at the gate let us in without asking many questions and I went straight to the Social Services Department, where I explained my problem with the lost luggage. They understood and promised that they would search their meagre supplies for some suitable things, which might fit my size and my needs. They would pack it into a suitcase and send it early in the morning to my barrack, before the transport was to assemble. They kept their word, and in the morning I received a paper suitcase crammed full with warm underwear, shirts and similar things. It stayed with me until the end of the war and the suitcase I keep still, as a souvenir of that time, though the contents are long gone.

Being in the middle of the night at the seat of self-administration, the authority that decided the fate of the individual, unless overridden by a specific direction of the SS command, was an opportunity not to be missed. My ghetto policeman had remained at the entrance gate where he chatted with the policeman on guard there, who happened to be his friend. I was, at least for some time, on my own and free to do whatever I wished. I decided first to make sure that I was on the list of participants of the transport. I went to the main registration office, where a number of girls were busy typing summons to the transport. Soon enough I found out I had guessed right and that my name was indeed on the list. What to do now? I had no acquaintance among the top people of the administration and of the lower echelons I knew only one, an engineer for whom I had done some technical work whilst still a student. Mr. K. was head of the technical services department, and I knew pretty well that he was my only chance. Incidentally, he is one of the very few members of the administration at that time who survived the camp.

I set out to search for him. I learned that he had been busy all day and the night before with preparations for leading the transport and that he was now exhausted and probably sleeping. With some persuasion and arm-twisting, I managed to find his room. In the camp there were no locks on the doors and thus I had no difficulty getting into his room. I found his bed and shook him awake. He recognized me and listened to my story, which he likely had already guessed. A period of silence ensued, probably only minutes, but to me it seemed like an eternity. Finally, he said:

"Look, my boy, I cannot do anything by myself. You have to find Mr.

Rust, the head of the electrical services department. His immediate superior is a German and that gives him some clout, although Mr. Rust is a civilian, not a soldier. He has been supervising the installation of electrical lighting at the site where the transport is to be loaded. Look to see if he is already back and bring him to me."

With that, I set out again, searching for Mr. Rust. Unfortunately, nobody had seen him and it appeared that he had not yet returned. In the meantime my ghetto policeman, my guardian angel, had become restless and began looking for me to deliver me to my barracks and perhaps go to bed as well. I tried to persuade him to give me a little more time, but he insisted that we had to return right away. Whilst that dispute was going on, a new person I had not noticed before showed up. He was wearing a heavy overcoat and had obviously come from outside. I asked my policeman for one last question, and turning to the newcomer I asked, "Have you seen Mr. Rust?"

Imagine my pleasant surprise when the answer came, "That's me. What can I do for you?"

"Please come with me to see Mr. K."

"Right now, in the middle of the night?"

"Yes, it is urgent, he is expecting us."

"Well, let's go."

The ghetto policeman did not dare object to the direction of a person of obviously higher rank and only said, "Don't stay too long, I'll wait for you here."

Mr. K. briefly explained to Mr. Rust my situation and added that I had studied three years of electrical engineering and, on top of that, had some experience in telephone exchanges. He said that I might be a useful addition to the staff. Mr. Rust had so far listened silently, even indifferently. Only when the word "telephone" came up, he became suddenly attentive. He asked questions, many questions... about my apprenticeship and my work at the small telephone company. Turning to Mr. K. he said:

"You know that the SS command plans to install a local telephone system which would connect to the Jewish self-administration, to the guard posts of the Czech gendarmes at the gates and even to some service establishments of the camp. But telephone technology is a rather specialized field. None of my present people have any experience in that field and I was afraid that before we could train somebody for it, we might run into a lot of dangerous trouble with the SS if maintenance problems arose. They are bound to occur mainly at the beginning. Your friend has come just at the right time. I will recommend him to the representative of the German Reichspost (postal service) who is in charge of all matters concerning this project. I do not doubt that he will accept my recommendation." Turning to me, he added:

"It is a good job you will have, provided you are up to its demands. It is risky, though. If you fail even once, your head may be at stake." And turning once again to Mr. K., he suggested:

"We cannot release him from the transport by ourselves. Let's go to the boss together."

By the boss he meant Mr. Edelstein, the head of the Jewish Council of Elders, the chief of the "autonomous" administration of the camp. So we trotted back again through the vast corridors of the Magdeburg barracks to Mr. Edelstein's office. I had to wait outside. Waiting was long and to say that I was worried would be the understatement of the year. My nervousness was certainly not alleviated by the menacing glances my "guardian angel" threw at me. He did not dare say anything, but was obviously afraid that he might be blamed for our late return.

Finally, my two protectors showed up again. Their faces were red and the discussion with Mr. Edelstein, and probably some of his advisors, had apparently been heated. They told me: "You go back to your barracks and pray. That's all we can say now!"

Though this reply was far from allaying my fears, it certainly gave me a glimmer of hope. The policeman and I, tramped back through the dark empty roads of the camp. The room at my barracks, which I shared with some forty others, mostly young men my age, was fully lit and busy. Nearly everybody seemed to be packing. I had nothing to pack and so I climbed to the third level of the bunk, which had been my bed for the last few weeks, threw myself on the straw-filled mattress fully dressed and waited. Perhaps I even prayed, I do not remember. It was a long wait.

It had been about midnight when I went back, and the messenger carrying the envelope with individual names came at about 5 a.m. I jumped down and ran to the sealed envelope, which was to be opened by the room elder. It had a 37 written on the outside in large red figures, but the seven had been crossed out and made into a six. I guessed, correctly as it turned out, that that was the number of summons the envelope contained. My hopes began to rise and reached a high point when the envelope was opened and my name was not on the list. However, it was not over yet.

About an hour later, the order came for the people of the transport to move to the improvised railway station where the transport was to be loaded. There they were counted apparently according to rooms. But the number of participants in each room which had been given to the group to organize and supervise the loading of the transport, the so-called "transport command", had apparently not been corrected.

After a while, a ghetto policeman appeared looking for the seemingly missing person. Fortunately, he did not have a name and though I knew quite well for whom he was looking I certainly did not volunteer and the room elder sent him away claiming that his quota had been filled. Anyway, I found this situation risky and decided to hide myself until the transport would be gone and the imminent danger disappeared. I was right, because as I was told afterwards, an hour or so later the policeman reappeared and asked for me by name, adding that he had been instructed to use force in case I would not go voluntarily.

Now, where to hide in a barrack with guards swarming all over the place? Only one place came to my mind. It was certainly not a pleasant one, but there seemed no better option. The latrine! Since the barracks where I had been assigned now contained many more people than they had been originally designed for, the number of latrines had to be increased by installing new ones. I knew of one that had been finished just the day before and probably had not yet been much used. That's where I went and sat with pants pulled down on an uncomfortable bar, shifting occasionally from place to place. Since the place was new, it was hardly frequented by anyone and nobody came looking for me. All the time I waited in the same uncomfortable position until I was fairly sure that the transport was gone before returning to my room. Finally the transport was really gone and everybody left in the camp was just happy to have survived another day so didn't bother to look for a missing participant.

The next day I received my instructions to go immediately to the building of the former post office where all telecommunication equipment was located, the only "exterritorial" building within the confines of the camp. There I was to report to the local representative of the German Reichspost, Mr. Habicht. After an interview of about an hour's duration, Mr. Habicht was satisfied and I was accepted as foreman of a newly to be established work commando of liner men, and for the moment, I was secure. My hungry years as an apprentice at "Prites", the small telephone company in Prague, had finally paid off and gradually became the key to my survival.

PLEASURES OF SS-SCHARFÜHRER HEINDL

SS-Scharführer (staff sergeant) Heindl was perhaps the most feared and detested of the SS guards with which we inmates occasionally came into contact. I was fortunate enough not to have a direct encounter with him. He was captured after the war, put to trial and sentenced to death for crimes against humanity.

According to Hitler's Nuremberg race laws, sexual relations between a member of the Aryan super race and a Jew were considered a crime. This law applied also to the Aryan male elite, the SS. Nonetheless, rumours had it that Heindl had a fancy for pretty young female prisoners, but for obvious reasons none of the involved girls dared talk about it. It was also commonly believed that girls who got pregnant or of whom he was tired were sent away in the next transport with the remark "return undesirable".

This is the story of one of Heindl's victims that I recount after so many years. It was told to me on the eve of her deportation to Auschwitz, knowing fully well of the death sentence accompanying her. The following text is the exact narration by that girl, except for some drastic and explicit details, which I preferred to leave out.

* * *

I was working in the agricultural commando, in a vast garden where vegetables and some fruits were grown for the table of the SS. It was a hot summer day and I was clothed only with the absolute minimum. All of a sudden, Heindl showed up ostensibly checking the harvest that was expected. There were a dozen girls working nearby, all similarly lightly clad, but his eyes fell on me. His stare made me feel uncomfortable and I tried to get away from him as much as I could, in vain. He beckoned me to follow him and went to a part of the garden, shaded by shrubs, where nobody was working. No inmate of the camp would resist the orders of an SS man. A beating with a riding whip Heindl used to carry would be the least punishment. He ordered, "Take off your blouse, I want to see what you have underneath."

The other girls may have noticed my disappearance, but would certainly be too afraid to follow us. In the summer heat, I had nothing under my blouse. Heindl came close and started to touch my breasts. I was frightened, but did not move. Then he lifted my skirt and placed his hand between my legs. I could see that he was pleased. He reached into his pocket and pulled out a permit that enabled the bearer to move freely within the walls of the ghetto at any time of the day or night. He gave me the card and told me, "At about 8 p.m. you make yourself, under some excuse, scarce and come to the guardhouse of gendarmes at gate number four. I will be waiting there for you. But not a word to anybody."

With this, he disappeared. I put on my blouse again and went back to my work. Some of the girls had seen me disappear and wanted to know what he had wanted and whether he had beaten me. I remembered the warning and said no, he just wanted to know how the raspberries were coming along.

In the evening, at the suggested time, I slipped out of our accommodation. My pass opened the door to the street with no questions asked. In hindsight, I strongly suspect that the guard at the gate knew something, though probably not everything about the matter. It was a strange feeling to walk alone through the empty streets. When I arrived at the meeting place, he was already waiting, but in civilian clothes, rather than in uniform. "You must not know where we are going, at least not yet today."

With that, he slipped a black ribbon over my eyes. He took me by the hand and we marched off at a fairly brisk pace. I tried to remember the direction we were taking but soon gave it up. Finally he stopped. I heard a key turning in a lock and we entered. He locked the door carefully behind us and then my blindfold was removed. I found myself in a dark corridor, closed by a door in front of us that he opened and we entered. We were in a spacious, well-lit room, equipped with furniture and a large bed, something I definitely would not have expected in the ghetto. Heavy blinds were on the windows and I later found out that the glass panes of the windows had been removed and replaced by plywood.

(Author's note: After the war, we found out that the place had been used by the intelligence service of the SS as a "safe house" for secret meetings with outside agents and occasionally their accommodation. There were indications that girls of Heindl's harem were sometimes offered to these agents. Rumours of a hidden torturing room could not be substantiated.)

Heindl then opened a side door that led to a well-equipped bathroom with the order, "Undress and have a bath. There is soap and toilet water. When you are finished, knock at the door. You don't have to dress. I want to see you naked. By the way, I hope you are not menstruating today."

Now we both knew that question was only a rhetorical one; we were all starving and the first thing the body of a starving woman does is stop menstruating. The bath was tempting though, I could not even remember the time I had my last one, and I filled the tub with pleasantly warm water and submerged myself into the warm embrace. Outside, Heindl had probably listened to the running of the water, because in a short time a girl came in, also in the nude, with a tray containing a slice of fresh bread, margarine and several slices of sausage - a luxurious meal for camp conditions. I devoured the food hastily and had just finished when the girl came in again to remove the tray. "I will now help to wash you," she said. I refused, saying I could wash myself.

"No, you don't know how. Let me show you and next time you can do it alone if you wish. Besides you would not know what to use today."

I considered that further resistance would be useless, so I gave in. In no time, she lathered me from head to toe. After rinsing it off, she rubbed some slightly fragrant oil into my skin. I had never before experienced a similar sensation.

When the procedure was finished, my companion led me back to the living room where I had been before. The first thing that my eyes fell on was Heindl, dressed only in underwear shorts. He definitely looked less formidable than in uniform. He was sitting in an armchair with a glass in his hands and a half-filled bottle beside him. Then there was a young boy, completely undressed, cowering in a corner and obviously frightened out of his wits. I felt almost certain that he was Jewish, an inmate of the camp like me, but I had no time to reflect. Heindl beckoned to me: "Come here; I want to inspect you as you are."

I Reluctantly approached him but he impatiently grabbed my shoulders and pulled me close. In no time, his hands were all over my body.

"Better than I had expected," he finally said. "Do you know why you are here?"

I shook my head.

"I want to make love to you. As long as you behave, you will be fed well and be certainly better off than the Jewish scum to which you belong. Otherwise..."

His tone was menacing, his voice almost a snarl. "Sit here next to me so I can touch your body whilst we are watching the spectacle." I was not sure what that meant, but it was clear that I had to obey.

"Start now with the show and do it well!" he ordered the girl who had been waiting on me. She obviously knew what was expected of her and did not need further instruction. Later I found out that the show, which was now to begin, was in its mildest form.

Upon that command, Sarah, as Heindl called her (I do not know if that was her true name) pulled the boy out of his corner where he was still shaking. The performance Heindl had previously mentioned began. Sarah knew well how to arouse Heindl and did her best job on the boy to satisfy her benefactor. That likely had been the purpose.

Then the two left the room, leaving me alone with the SS man. Watching Heindl's reaction, I knew what was coming. ... Suddenly he lifted me up like a feather and threw me on the prepared bed and a moment later, he was lying on top of me, smothering me with his well-fed body. I was gasping for air. ...

It did not last very long but to me it seemed like an eternity. ... When he finished, he threw me out of the bed to the floor, kicked me with his bare feet, and shouted, "Get out of this bed, you Jewish whore, get dressed and disappear. I'll let you know when I need your body again." Then, more mildly, he said, "It was nice with you and I am sure that it will be quite often especially after you have learned your job."

That was my first encounter with that beast and many more followed until he found a replacement. Not all the following episodes with him were that nonviolent; quite the contrary.

Since that day, my life in the ghetto changed. I was transferred to the planning group of the gardening commando, where in the summer I had nothing to do. I received supplementary ration cards so I was not starving anymore and at my visits to the safe house, which I could now walk to alone, I always got some rare food supplements, once, I remember even chocolate.

However, improved nourishment brought back my menstruation and, with that, the danger of becoming pregnant with deportation as consequence if I could not get an abortion before it was discovered. Now, in hindsight, I know that my present fate was to be expected.

One day I received a notice to come at the usual hour to the usual place. I showed up as many times before, and had my bath, by now alone. When I re-entered the living room, there it was again; Sarah and a boy. I hadn't seen him before. Heindl was there in his armchair as usual, but he seemed nervous. The opening was the customary one. Sarah played with the boy and made love to him for Herr Heindl's pleasure, which was by now for me routine. Then, everything went differently. The love play performed for him did not elicit Heindl's usual ecstatic reaction, just the opposite. When I tried to be helpful, he pushed me roughly away.

"Bring in the bench", he finally shouted to Sarah. The boy seemed to know what that meant, because he became pale and began to tremble. What Sarah then brought in was a small bench attached to a wooden plank, perhaps one metre long, which had some leather belts attached to the far end. She ordered the boy to kneel down on that plank and to place his chest on that bench at the other end. Then she used belts to fix his chest and legs, with the legs somewhat apart. From a drawer Sarah produced a whip with a long thin leather thong attached to it.

Then Sarah told me, "Now look at me, I'll teach you how to do it. You have to beat him on the buttocks and on the lower part of his back. Occasionally he asks me to hit his testicles. You must not be too mild when beating, otherwise you might find yourself in his place, and your soft smooth skin will be gone forever."

After these words, she swung the whip with what appeared to be full force and the thin cord painted a red streak across the white buttocks of the boy. Another blow and then another followed. The skin began to burst and blood oozed out. Then she handed the whip to me. "Try it."

I did not find it easy at all. I did not want to hurt the boy, who was already groaning too much, but was also afraid of what might happen to me. After a few blows, rather weak ones, Sarah indicated that I have to beat more violently and try to hit his crotch. The end of the thong hit the target and a terrible scream ensued. It seemed to have an electrifying effect on the SS man; he jumped up, snatched the whip out of my hands and started blindly to beat with full force. Blood was all over the boy's body. It seemed to have a magic effect upon Heindl. ... He pounced on the boy and raped him.

When he finally finished with his screaming victim, he administered a last heavy blow and from a coaster I had not noticed before rubbed salt into the wounds and sat back into his armchair enjoying the agony of the boy.

Finally, we got permission to untie him and to wash the salt from his wounds. I did not see the boy again. I presume his fate was about the same that is now awaiting me. He went with the transport and disappeared. Whether he survived, I don't know, but I doubt it.

Episodes of that kind took place periodically about once a month. Sarah and I had to attend always. She will probably continue to do her job after I am gone. Only the boys always change. Just one boy I saw twice. Perhaps Heindl could not find a suitable victim. The second time the boy, of course, knew what to expect and was shaking with fear. He then disappeared as all before him.

STRATEGIC MICA

After the evacuation transport in the fall of 1942, the number of inmates of the ghetto had shrunk to a minimum. All production facilities had come to a halt even though they were mostly serving the armed forces. The reason was simple; virtually all their labour force was gone. Only one remained intact and was actually enlarged significantly – workshops for the splitting of mica. The resulting thin sheets were to be used for high voltage insulators in electronic equipment, presumably radar. We did not know that at the time and I doubt that anybody in the camp knew what radar was all about.

The mineral, muscovite, was brought to the camp in large blocks as they came from the mine. Blocks were cut by machine into smaller lumps that were given to a large number of women whose task was to split them into thin sheets. The work took place in a long wooden hall built specifically for that purpose. There was little to no artificial ventilation and the air was heavy with dust. A woman who would have worked here for a prolonged time would certainly have attracted silicosis or a serious lung disease. Of course, the health of their slave workers was the least of the concerns of the SS command.

At that time, I had a ghetto "wife" and our improvised marriage had saved us both from the transport and certain end. The kitchens where she had worked for the last two years were much too large for the much smaller crowd they now had to feed and much of their personnel was discharged, my wife among them. Most of the, now redundant, kitchen personnel had been disposed of in the previous large liquidation transports. My narrow escape from one of these I have described in a story of my lost luggage. According to ghetto rules, if a husband was safe from transport, his wife would be protected, as well. I knew that the degree of protection from transports I had enjoyed up to now, if it persisted at all, was weak and that we both stood a good chance to go with the next transport.

Now, the SS command had given the mica production highest priority and indicated that workers employed there would be safe from further transports. Nobody placed too much confidence into promises of the SS, too many had already been broken. However, at least it offered a glimmer of safety, however unreliable, which was better than nothing. In any case, nothing safe seemed to be available. There was one promise from the SS, which had more or less been kept; that families wouldn't be separated. If my wife would enjoy some degree of protection, I might benefit from that as well.

With that in mind, I tried my best to secure her a place in the mica workshops, despite the tough conditions I knew she would have to face. The promise of protection had spread quickly and women were desperate for a place. Difficulties I expected, but what I met was beyond my wildest expectations. Whether somebody intervened finally on my behalf, I do not know. I presume, however, that must have been the case. Anyway, after many fruitless attempts and weeks of anxious waiting, she got finally the longed for white transfer papers, assigning her to the mica shop.

Hard times were ahead, though. Whilst she had been working in the kitchen, we had escaped the worst hunger. Although we would never dare take anything out of the kitchen, which would buy a culprit a ticket to Auschwitz if caught, there was a chance for her to find a morsel to eat in the kitchen. In addition, when she was on duty I could have part and sometimes the whole of her ration card for myself. That all stopped now, but we had a chance to survive and that was all that counted. Hungry times were ahead for both of us. When Germany finally collapsed, I weighed slightly more than 40 kilograms. With her, it was not much better. Still, she managed to endure hunger, shift work, humiliation and abuse till the very end and we both survived.

THE MAN FROM LODŹ

It was a warm midsummer day in 1942 when I got an emergency call that the telephone in the office of his highness, the camp commander, was out of order and that he demanded it fixed as fast as possible. Now my custom on such an occasion was first to check at the exchange, whether the fault was not there. Inevitably the next step was a check of the lines, where the majority of faults occurred. For understandable reasons, the office of the boss of bosses was the last place I wanted to go. Unfortunately, in that case I had no choice.

I reported at the entrance of the former hotel, which was now occupied by camp command, where I got my permit and the usual guard to accompany me. When I entered the office, the commander was in conversation with another SS officer whom I had not seen before. I was a nobody and they did not bother to interrupt their conversation or even to lower their voices. They had a pile of photographs on the table in front of them and were laughing and joking whilst looking at them. I could overhear much, though not everything of their conversation and occasionally caught a glance at the pictures spread on the table. I soon gathered that the newcomer was a visitor from the ghetto of Lodź, a city in Poland.

Before the Theresienstadt ghetto was established, a number of transports from Prague had gone to the Lodź ghetto, so the name was not altogether unfamiliar to me. What I heard him saying about Lodź was not very inviting but not much worse than what I had heard before. He was also relaying something else, about the numerous small camps that were apparently dotting the Polish countryside. Much of his talk was illustrated by photos and the gist of his account seemed to be advice to the local SS about the best way of achieving the "final solution". Of course, I had only fleeting glances at the displayed pictures, but the vivid description, which accompanied them, described in many cases what the eye was missing.

I remember a picture apparently taken from high up, showing an open field covered with bodies, with rows of others still standing in the background. From his commentaries, it was evident that the lying bodies were people from the Lodź ghetto who had been mowed down by machine guns mounted on the spire of the village church. Those standing in the background were waiting for their turn. Another photo showed a group of people, perhaps a dozen or so, with nooses over their necks and the ends of ropes passing over hooks on a wooden crossbar to the rear end of a truck, which when moving forward would lift them from the ground. There was a photo showing a man, his hands tied backwards to his feet and with head down, hanging by his knees on a bar. The picture showed an SS man standing before the man with a foot raised and apparently about to kick him in the face.

The visitor described a woman being tortured to death by giving her an enema with boiling hot water, and another one where pressurized water was used until her intestines were bursting. I remember him saying, "Liquidating the vermin is easy, but to get rid of their stinking bodies is a problem, there are just too many. We are now about to build a large compound that will replace the small, uneconomic places. Everything will be streamlined using the most up-to-date factory techniques. Liquidation, transportation of the corpses to the disposal site and final disposal will be taken care of in one highly mechanized unit. In less than a year, it will go into operation and our work will then become so much easier."

I was torn between two urges: to work slowly so that I could hear and see more, and to hasten up before the SS men became aware of my presence and of the possibility that I might have overheard much of what had been said. Perhaps they did not mind that or even had intended it as a kind of psychological torture. Anyway, I was let go once the repair was finished and nobody spoke further to these events. Naturally, I was shaken and frightened. To keep my mouth shut about what I had seen and heard seemed to be the safest response.

Several months later, a confirmation arrived. A young member of the electrical department, a good friend of mine, had been selected for one of the almost continuous series of transports for resettlement in the East. A few weeks later arrived one of those pre-printed 30 word cards the transport victims were sometimes allowed to send. It was signed, "Sincere greetings from your friend Plyn." Of course, his name was not Plyn. Plyn is a Czech word and means "gas." It was clear, to me at least, that those who were in the picture now knew the meaning of the word "resettlement". What I had overheard in the commander's office was no idle talk.

MINUTES FROM EXECUTION

In early 1942 the telephone system of the ghetto was just in its infancy and the office of the camp commander was forcefully pushing for its rapid completion. A special construction outfit, or "Baukommando" in German was established and I was put in charge as its foreman. We had been busy installing hooks along the walls of the buildings of the old town and wooden poles in open areas to support the telephone wires. Though none of us had any previous experience in that kind of work, in the course of several months, we learned it the hard way. Of course, we were always under the watchful eyes of Mr. Habicht of the Reich postal services, detached to the ghetto for that purpose, and of a gendarme of the Czech guards.

We had just completed our "learning" period and considered ourselves "experts" in this kind of work, when the news came that a "Sonderkommando", a special SS outfit, had been transferred to our area and had temporarily pitched camp not too far from the "Small Fortress". At that time, we were not aware of the sinister connotation of the term, "Sonderkommando".

Therefore, we were not particularly alarmed.

Shortly after their arrival I was called to our boss Mr. Habicht, and told the unit was awaiting orders from higher up. Therefore, they were in urgent need of a wire link to the long distance exchange. That exchange was located in a building that was now in the middle of the ghetto. Because of the large volume of traffic expected, and also to ensure against possible eavesdropping, a multi-wire aerial cable should be used instead of the usual open wire lines. We were ordered to build a line for that purpose in the shortest possible time, even if it meant working 24 hours a day. I was given a sketch of the course the line was to take to avoid built-up areas and given first priority on any of the already scarce material that might be needed. I also received permission to recruit any number of support workers who might be needed.

Now, an overhead cable contains many individual thin wires in a metal and plastic sheathing. It is very heavy, too heavy to span the 100 feet or so between poles without support. A steel cable strung between adjacent poles provides that support. Clamps about three feet apart suspend the main cable from the supporting wires.

Several long and tiring days later the construction was completed, the line put into operation and the episode was all but forgotten. However, a few weeks later we were reminded of it in a rather crude way, when a heavy storm hit the area during the night. At the usual "Appell", all members of the working group involved in the construction of the line were collected by grim looking SS men we did not know and carted away on a waiting truck.

I myself was marched between two SS men to the office of our exchange. Why I was given such honour I cannot say. Perhaps I was regarded as the ringleader of the alleged conspiracy and singled out for interrogation, but no investigation happened. The SS had already decided upon a course of action and further investigation was deemed unnecessary.

At the exchange, a group of SS officers were assembled. Some of them I knew from the camp, others I had never seen before. As usual, my presence was ignored and the conversation that had been going on continued. Listening to it, I discovered that during the storm the night before the suspension wire of the cable of the new line had snapped and the cable it carried had broken. The special unit was expecting some urgent instructions and was hopping mad at the loss of communication. They had examined the breakage and came to the conclusion that an act of sabotage was involved with the only possible perpetrator being people from our group. To be sure, they had already in the early morning hours brought in some experts from the nearest communication centre of the Protectorate. These people, afraid for their own skin, had wholeheartedly confirmed their suspicion. On these grounds, they had approached the SS command of the camp to release us to them for "exemplary treatment".

"Our" SS had obviously been reluctant to accede to that demand. Not that they had pity for the fate that would have certainly awaited us at the hands of the Sonderkommando. The true reason was that we were already considered to be experts and that other work had already been scheduled for us; work that was urgently needed and the execution of which was now threatened. There were also instructions from Berlin that Theresienstadt was to be a "show ghetto". Any cases of "special treatment" were to be carried out at the "Small Fortress" or at camps in the East. In the end, a compromise was found. We were simply to be shot clandestinely with no "deterrent special treatment" (read public torture). We were just to disappear and some excuse would be found to explain that. Everything was already arranged and only a few paper formalities remained.

The situation appeared hopeless. Suddenly, I heard a car pulling up in front of the building. Now a car in a concentration camp is certainly not commonplace and the group fell silent waiting for the passengers of the car to come up the stairs. And he came. It was nobody else than Mr. Engling, my former boss from Prague, the "Aryan" trustee of the small telephone company who had sheltered me for as long as he could. He was in civilian attire, but from the respectful way he was greeted I gathered that he must be in a quite high position. If he recognized me, he did not show it. I can only guess whether he came just by chance or whether he had already received some information about what was going on in the ghetto. Anyway, he arrived literally in the last minute.

Ignoring my presence, he started to banter and then asked for the reason of that gathering. He was told that there had been an act of sabotage and that the perpetrators of the act were now to face the consequences. Upon hearing that Engling asked for more details and then requested to see the scene of the incident. The men from the special unit scowled and objected, saying that our guilt was proven and that the lives of a few Jews were not worth his time and attention. However, Engling insisted, claiming it was a matter of principle, and the SS gave in.

The whole company boarded cars and with me loaded into the back of one they drove off to the place of the mishap. Our unexpected visitor inspected the broken end of the carrying wire long and carefully. After a long pause he calmly declared, "I see no evidence of sabotage. This is wartime material. There is a large insertion piece that has reduced the strength of the material and caused it to break during the storm. It would have broken sometime later anyway. There was no act of sabotage."

The SS people were not pleased with his views and showed it quite openly. They objected, as all the paperwork had been done and all arrangements for the "final solution" been completed. "We have spent hours on them and whether they bite the grass earlier or later is not so important. They will eventually be liquidated anyway. So why not finish the job right away?" However, Engling retorted calmly: "How to proceed with these people is your business and you are free to do as you wish. But I have to caution you. These guys have been doing their jobs for many months and they know how to go about it. To familiarize new people with that work will take again many months. Mr. Habicht is needed for more important duties and will be called off in the next few weeks. Who then is going to train the new crew and to oversee their work? I had to relinquish most of my experienced personnel for the Eastern front and I am stripped to the bone. From me, you cannot expect to get any replacement for Mr. Habicht, even temporarily. For the foreseeable future you have to make do with what you have. But the decision is up to you."

I was quite surprised to see that the ghetto SS men were nodding in agreement. At this moment, some of the Sonderkommando seemed to perceive my presence. A hint to the two SS men who had guarded me all this time and I was dragged out of earshot, but could see that a lively discussion went on for quite a while.

When it seemed that it had ended, I was loaded into a truck and driven to the execution place in the Small Fortress. Upon arrival there, I saw the fellows of the construction crew who had been hauled away by the SS in the morning, had already been blindfolded and tied to poles. Several SS men of the Sonderkommando were lying in the grass some 50 feet away: drinking, smoking, and playing cards. The significance of their presence was underlined by two machine guns mounted in firing position. I had only seconds to take in the picture of that scene before being blindfolded, as well and tied to one of the remaining poles. It was about eleven o'clock in the morning when I arrived; the other fellows had been standing there since about eight o'clock.

These were long hours; the sun was burning and from time to time, the SS fired a few shots over our heads presumably so that we should not feel bored. Having witnessed the arrival of Mr. Engling and the ensuing discussion, I had gained some hope. Not so the others, who were expecting at any moment the bullets to be aimed a little lower so as to crush our heads. Even for me these were long, long hours. Finally, when the sun was already setting, we were untied. The blindfolds were removed and we were all loaded into a truck to bring us back "home". As a farewell, we were given the final warning: "Today we have shown mercy. Next time we might be in a different mood, so behave!"

The news of us being carted away in the morning had spread like a wildfire through the ghetto. Nobody had actually expected that we might come back. This would have certainly not happened had Mr. Engling arrived a few minutes later. Did he know and come on purpose? Was it chance? A merciful Providence? We will never know. Mr. Engling was killed by a mob in the streets of Prague during the Prague uprising in 1945.

HOW I MET MY DEAD FATHER

To explain the headline and put it straight, I should remind the reader that I had lost both my parents very early and was adopted by my father's brother who is the central figure of this episode. He was my stepfather but I loved him as my true father. He was not married, but had a housekeeper, an elderly lady. I call her auntie here, but she was like mother to me and treated me as her own child.

When the Sudetenland, including Postoloprty, was annexed by Hitler's Germany, every person living there had to decide overnight – either to remain here as Germans, or leave as a Czech. I decided to leave and my uncle refused. His arguments were, "I am liked by everyone here, I have no enemies, I am more German than Czech, so nothing will happen to me." My auntie did not want to leave him. It was a big mistake, which cost them their lives.

Initially, a few mixed families that stayed supported them by secretly bringing them food and things the German shopkeeper refused to sell. As German rule became more established, fewer people had the courage, and eventually they stopped helping altogether.

Several months later, the local super Nazi submitted a petition that they wanted the town to become "Judenrein", meaning "Clean of Jews". The petition was granted and, after some delay, the remaining Jews of Postoloprty were shipped to the provisional mini-camp in Edersgrün (Odeř), which had been established just for that purpose.

It must have happened a few months before my deportation, because the letters stopped arriving. My auntie died before her deportation and local Nazis did not even allow her to be buried in the Jewish cemetery of the town. Her body was probably interred in a mass grave near Měcholupy, where a vacant field was destined to serve as cemetery for any Jews that had the audacity to die in a country reserved for the pure race.

I do not know much about living conditions at the camp where my uncle was deported, what happened there before the second deportation, or how many, if any, internees remained there or whether the camp was at that time completely liquidated. I believe it was in the second half of 1942 when my uncle and another neighbour from Postoloprty were transferred from the Edersgrün camp to a ghetto in Terezín.

Anyway, the administration of the ghetto knew that a transport from Edersgrün was to arrive the other day and they even knew the names of the participants. Somebody in the administration also knew that my adoptive father was interned in that camp, and when he saw the name on the list of arrivals guessed that it might be him. Whatever the reasons, I was advised of the place where the transport was to be received. Small transports like this were not channelled through the transit barracks, the Schleuse, where inmates were inspected and disinfected.

I arrived at that place just in time to witness the unloading of the newcomers, but I did not see a familiar face. When all of them had disembarked, two male nurses of the sanitary service of the ghetto boarded the car and carried out two lifeless bodies. One of them was my stepfather, the other one his companion from Postoloprty. They placed the two bodies on the floor and I was allowed to come close. My stepfather was emaciated and if I had not known about his impending arrival, I would have had difficulty recognizing him. The other body had a similar appearance. Talking to the other people of the transport, I was told that both had been alive and appeared normal when they boarded the car. During the voyage they had apparently fallen asleep, a sleep from which they were not to awaken.

It was sad, but at that time I had no suspicion. I really believed that they had both succumbed to the exertions of the camp and that their old bodies, weakened by months of starvation, could not be sustained anymore. Only much later I learned that they had succumbed to poison, administered by their own hand. Or, were they given the poison by someone else, perhaps with food or water? There were also rumours that the poison was intended for somebody else and the two had fallen victim to a fatal mistake. Neither of the two had any luggage, just the clothes they were wearing. This could be taken as a sign that they were not thinking of spending any time in the ghetto. It was equally possible that some fellow passengers simply took possession of their belongings once it was found they were dead. I have never found out the truth.

EVERYDAY GHETTO LIFE

Life in Theresienstadt was, for the average inmate, comparable to life in a maximum-security prison. This concerns only security. As far as creature comfort goes, a prison of that kind in the Western world would seem a deluxe hotel in comparison to the camp.

However unpleasant and disagreeable the lack of creature comfort was, it was not the main factor that made camp life so hard to bear. Far more depressing was the slow but continuous starvation. Older and weaker people succumbed to that insidious method sometimes in a few months, and rarely survived a full year. Before the camp crematorium was built, the dead, mostly older people were buried in unmarked mass graves. I remember the winter of 1942/43 when the ground was solidly frozen and too hard for grave digging, frozen corpses piled up two metres high in a stack just inside the walls.

Younger people survived but were getting more and more emaciated. After the war, when I was drafted to military service, I weighed in at forty kilograms, almost half my previous weight. Besides, from the very beginning, all of us suspected that "resettlement" in the East would lead to living conditions which would be significantly worse than the ones experienced in Theresienstadt.

NEWS SEEPS IN AND AROUND

As time went by, news of the real meaning of "resettlement" began to trickle in and progressed slowly from rumour to certainty. Details, of course, were not known. Though some of the rumours were exaggerated, they did not do justice to the full horror of Auschwitz and other death camps. One never knew whether the next day would bring the dreaded message of deportation by the next transport. This amounted to psychological torture. I even suspect that the SS spread some of the circulating rumours via their stool pigeons to keep the psychological pressure going. That was not difficult, since transports were leaving in irregular intervals, but never stopped completely. Incoming transports became gradually less frequent as there were fewer and fewer people left to be deported.

Less successful was the attempt of the SS to keep the camp in the dark about the progress of the war. Although contact with the civilian population in the areas surrounding the camp was minimal, some news continued to trickle in that way. By being passed on by word of mouth, they were inevitably distorted until they had very little in common with the original news. Another important source of information was the new arrivals who were coming in small groups, almost continuously. Naturally, the news they brought in was also propagated by word of mouth and suffered the same distortion and exaggeration.

My main preoccupation, the telephone system, brought with it the opportunity to listen, in unguarded moments, to telephone conversations... not only local ones, but in rare instances also long distance ones. These were, of course, the most interesting. Since nobody suspected that these conversations could be overheard, the talkers, mainly officers of the SS or security service SD, did not always guard themselves and sometimes spoke more freely than normally.

I had another productive source of information as well. At that time, direct long distance dialing was not yet in vogue and all long distance calls had to be channelled through operators at either end. The long distance operators of the camp were German girls. Long distance traffic was not very intense and so the girls were passing the time with all kind of needlework, whilst a radio was running full blast. That I was working next door, in the room where the exchange machinery was located, did not disturb them. For them, as for anybody else of our "hosts", I was a nobody, well on the path to oblivion, so they were not concerned that I could hear everything the loudspeaker blared, including Dr. Goebbel's (the propaganda minister of the Thousand Year Reich) latest "news". However, sometimes there was a core of truth in them. I can still remember the terse announcement:

"The enemy has last night begun the attack on Sicily with strong naval and air formations. The battle is continuing."

Many months later I overheard a similar, still weightier announcement only a day or two after it actually happened. It was a message downplaying as an insignificant diversion the landing of the Western Allies at the coast of Normandy. For a relatively short time I was also privy to another source of information: a clandestine radio receiver, with which we were able to listen to the late night news of the BBC. The fate of that device is briefly described in another episode of this collection. It had taken a year to assemble parts and build the device. Unfortunately, its useful life was much shorter than that. It had to be destroyed out of fear it might be discovered by the SS.

I was probably, for much of the time, one of the best-informed people in the ghetto. However, knowing the news was one thing. Spreading it was quite another. The news was given only to a narrow circle of carefully selected people and then only with a delay of one or more days. Wherever possible, the available information was broken down into fragments. Each fragment was given to a different person. The messages passed on in that way made sense only when a number of these fragments could be combined. The idea was, of course, to make it difficult to trace the source of the news even in the ever-present danger of leaks, either usually unintentional or deliberate. The original members in our news propagation chain were carefully selected and certainly reliable. However, every so often one member of that chain was lost to a transport and had to be replaced. There used to be little time for thorough checks and the danger of leaks and betrayal became gradually larger. Generally, the system worked. Though there were traces of occasional leaks, the SS never managed to break the system and find the source from where much of the information that circulated in the ghetto emanated. If they had succeeded, none of us at the top of the news pyramid would have survived the next transport.

A CHRISTMAS GIFT

My boss in the early days of the ghetto, Mr. Habicht, was a civilian employee of the "Reichspost". He was a member of the Nazi party of course. Otherwise, he would not have been assigned to work in a concentration camp. To be fair, I have to say that he certainly was not a fanatic for whom Hitler's *Mein Kampf* was gospel and Jews the cause of all evil. He was living in a roomy apartment on the third floor of the exchange building in the middle of the ghetto, and was probably its only non-Jewish inhabitant. He never wore a uniform, only a swastika badge on his lapel. Since the inmates in Theresienstadt did not wear the striped concentration camp pyjamas, to the casual observer only that badge could identify him as a member of the master race. I remember, in that regard, an episode that normally would have been funny, but could have had serious consequences if somebody else had been involved.

The telephone system of the ghetto used bare wires strung on insulators mounted on the walls of the buildings. One stretch of these wires went along the Dresden barracks, where women were accommodated. Men were not allowed in without a special pass. Now, the women there had a habit of using the telephone wires under their windows as a clothesline for their laundry. The results were short circuits that put the system out of operation. The barrack elder had been warned several times to put a stop to that practice, but in vain.

Once a short circuit happened again and complaints about the telephone system not functioning came rushing in. Mr. Habicht got angry and decided to attend to the matter himself. With me in his tow, he marched to the site of the problem. The first problem arose at the gate. The policeman on duty kept asking for a pass we did not have. Luckily, he remained polite and did not try to be rough. When he finally noticed the swastika badge, he almost fainted and let us in with a hundred apologies.

We went up the stairs to the room that we had estimated had laundry hung up from the window. When we opened the door, we saw some thirty-odd young women scantily clad or completely naked, hopping around. When they saw two men entering the room many of them tried to cover themselves with whatever piece of fabric was in reach. However, two or three of them threw themselves upon us, embracing us and pressing their bodies against us in an obvious invitation to reciprocity. Habicht, who had been the first to enter the room, was obviously embarrassed. He tried to fend off the probing hands of the women without hurting them. Only when they noticed the swastika did they let up and then fled to the farthest corner of the room. Habicht then went to the window without paying further attention to them, pulled the laundry pieces from the wire and left, barking only, "For the last time." I don't have to say that I followed him, thanking

God that he had not reacted differently.

I don't know whether Habicht was married or not. What I knew was that he had a girlfriend, a Czech woman from a city not too far from Prague. That lady came to see him, usually once a month, and stayed with him in his apartment in the ghetto. We were quite amused by that audacity, because we knew that the SS was trying to seal the ghetto off as much as they could from visits by outside persons. I suspect that Habicht's violation of that ordinance was one of the reasons why he had lost his safe and comfortable job in the ghetto and been transferred to other duties. It is true that with the visits of Miss S. he was taking quite a risk.

Aside from the visits of his girlfriend, he was more than cautious. It was shortly before Christmas in 1942 that his girlfriend showed up again with a big bag that we assumed contained Christmas gifts. Although the Germans in the camp were well fed, she had brought some homemade delicacies as a change from the monotony of the regular canteen food. She obviously wanted to give some of it to us but did not dare do it openly, so a ruse was employed.

On Christmas Eve, I was called to Mr. Habicht's office for instructions. His girlfriend was also present. Several dishes were neatly arranged in the office and the two had obviously already been eating from them. There was also a hearty piece of schnitzel between two slices of fresh bread arranged on a sheet of white paper. When I received my instructions and was being dismissed, she seemingly inadvertently pulled that paper from the desk and the goodies fell to the floor. She pretended to pick it up when he intervened. "We won't eat from the floor, darling." Turning to me he said, "Pick up that mess and throw it into a garbage can."

He knew of course perfectly well that that piece of garbage was for us and that it would certainly not end up in a trash can. Indeed, after sharing with my companion, (our group consisted at that time only of two persons) and reserving part for my wife, I had, after many months, a full stomach. I can assure you that that simple meal tasted better than had many a sumptuous dinner before or after the war.

WELL-CONCEALED RADIO

At some point in late 1943, Mr. Bobek, the German boss of the department of electrical services of the ghetto had come to the conclusion that it would be best to concentrate the living quarters of the all-male personnel of his department into one building. The Jewish administration of the camp didn't like the idea, but there was little they could do about it. A medium sized house near the main square was selected and its occupants distributed among other lodgings, and we moved in. At the entrance a room had been set aside as a kind of guard chamber. There an emergency service was installed which was staffed all day and night. To serve its purpose, the room was equipped with a supply of spare parts, tools, and measuring instruments. There was also a couch where the men on night duty could relax and, in the early morning hours when things used to be quiet, could catch a few hours of sleep.

My main business was the telephone system, its maintenance and installation. However, since I had become a member of the electrical department, I had to do all kinds of other jobs, from repairing a hot plate to the installation of floodlights at the rail yard. Not quite official, but even more important, were all kinds of similar services for the SS, with the repair of record players and radio receivers a sizeable part of that work. The SS used all conceivable means to prevent any information leaks about what was going on in the world. News trickled in anyway, but was often distorted. A radio receiver in the ghetto was an unthinkable possibility. When I had to fix one of these gadgets, I was under the strictest of supervision and control by an SS guard. Of course, for doing this kind of work you need spare parts. Most of them are quite small and could easily be hidden in an inconspicuous place. Patiently collecting these parts for a period of a year or so, I had sufficient material to build a crude, simple but working receiver. In the wee hours of the morning, even the BBC could be received.

Of course, I knew the risks and the danger if caught, but sometimes I took it on the light shoulder. The device was hidden under a switching panel in the wall of our ready room where a brick had been removed. My telephone test set served as an earphone, and screws that appeared to attach the panel to the wall were used for tuning. Of course, I could not have done all that by myself without the help of a few trustworthy friends. This made us the best-informed people in the ghetto. There were strict rules about passing on this information to other prisoners. Unfortunately, the news spread somehow and reached the SS, who had, of course, its stool pigeons among the inmates. In hindsight, that was inevitable and I can only wonder that it took so long to happen.

Anyway, the SS got a tip about a secret radio receiver somewhere in the ghetto and tried to locate it in the usual way, by measurement. Fortunately, the very crudeness of the design of our receiver prevented them from locating it, but they apparently had some vague information about its location. Whether it was a traitor's information or a lucky guess, we did not find out. One early morning, I happened to be on duty in the ready room when a squad of SS men burst in, brandishing their side arms, submachine guns and the like. One of them placed the nozzle of his pistol on my forehead and shouted, "Where is that radio, you Jewish pig?" I pretended to tremble, and probably did, and returned in a broken voice, in German,

"A radio, here? I never heard of anything."

"Talk fast, or I pull the trigger", was the reply.

He pushed the gun more and more into my face and I became afraid he would push it into my eyes. I did not know what they really knew or if they were bluffing, but I knew only too well that if they found it, it would be the end of all of us, and not a smooth end at all. So, I gathered what courage was left in me and replied with as firm a voice as I could manage, "You must be mistaken. Here, nobody would dare such a thing, Captain."

Of course, he was no captain but he seemed to like the way I addressed him. He pulled back his gun and ordered his men to make a thorough search of the house. Fortunately, the panel, behind which the radio was hidden, with all its instruments, sockets, and switches, looked so real and innocent that they did not pay attention to it. The search lasted perhaps three hours and the ghetto went about its daily routine when they left without having found anything. Their interrogations had not produced any results either. The few people who knew, knew also what was at stake and kept their tongues. We were all frightened. We knew the SS would continue to be on the alert and might come back. Therefore, we all decided reluctantly to destroy the set the next night when one of us would be on duty. The SS did not come back, and we lost our best source of information, but all of us breathed a bit easier.

WEDDING

"Heydrich is dead!" He was assassinated by a command unit sent by the Czechoslovak government in exile in London and the news had reached the Gestapo who were out for revenge. Mass executions, more transports! The ghetto was abuzz with rumours, some substantiated, some not. I don't know how they penetrated so fast the supposedly impenetrable border to the outside world, but they were there with more and more detailed accounts every day. Whatever plans the Gestapo had for revenge, nobody had any doubts that many of them would turn against the eternal culprit, the Jews. And turn against us they did.

One transport crammed with its human cargo arrived from the vicinity of Prague. It was not even allowed to unload; all of the transport had "Weisung", the death sentence. Then news arrived of another transport, this time from the capital. It also had "Weisung", but was supposed to stay several nights in Theresienstadt, before continuing to the gas chambers of Majdanek. Nobody knew why the short stop. Perhaps the German transport system to the East was overloaded.

Ahead of the transport arrived a list with the names of the victims. Again the question: why? On the list were the names of the family of my girlfriend from Prague. We had met by accident. I have already mentioned that we were living in the same house and since Jews were not allowed into the streets after eight o'clock, we became fast friends, and then lovers. I do not remember anymore how I learned about their arrival, but I got the message ahead of time, which was crucial. I reflected on what to do to save them. That they were destined to die I knew for certain. So I decided to use my newly acquired possibility to move, at least during day time, freely around the ghetto to inquire at the central administration in the Magdeburg barracks about any possibilities. The answers were disappointing. Nobody was prepared to interfere on behalf of one of the sacrificial lambs for the great SS general. I was already giving up, when the head of the central evidence told me:

"I cannot do anything for the parents or for your girl's sister, but why don't you marry her? I know you love her, and it's the only chance. Mind you, you run a risk. German policy is, for the time being at least, to keep families together. When you marry her, you will become a family and either stay together or go together. Chances are about equal. Make up your mind fast. There is not much time to spare."

I have to admit we had never talked about marriage. Nor would I have married her under normal conditions, we were too different personalities. I knew I could not let her die without even lifting a finger, and there was no other choice. Without even thinking how much was at stake for me, because in my new position I knew that I was safe; I simply said yes.

"I hope you know what you are doing and I hope still more that you will get away with it. Now we have to see the boss, Mr. Edelstein. I can't make such a decision."

Then we went to Mr. Edelstein's office and he tried hard to talk me out of it. I don't know whether he was serious or whether he just wanted to test my sincerity. After a lengthy discussion during which I resisted changing my intentions, he finally said, "I admire you. I will do what you want." Then he went with me to the chief rabbi to arrange for the wedding to take place immediately after the arrival of the train.

The train arrived late at night and the people were accommodated in the transit barracks, the "Schleuse". I managed to squeeze among the people from the transport and soon discovered the people I was looking for. I had to tell them not what was in store for them, but only that they were supposed to continue after only a day or so, further east. Then I told the father that I intended to marry his daughter the next morning and that she would, hopefully, stay with me whilst they would have to go. I don't remember in detail her father's reaction anymore, but he seemed to be content. The mother's reaction came as a shock to me.

"I know," she said, "the risk you are taking and I admire you for that. I hope you will both manage to survive. If that happens, don't feel tied by what you are doing now. You are such different persons and maybe each of you will be happier with a different partner."

I had reported in my barracks that I might not come back that night and since everybody knew what was going on, there were no objections.

We passed the night together lying on the cold floor tiles of the ancient building, which were covered only with a thin layer of straw. There was not much sleep for any of us, each occupied with own thoughts, fears and hopes.

The wedding ceremony had been scheduled for early morning, because nobody knew when the transport would be loaded again. The chief rabbi of the ghetto performed the ceremony, and despite the sparse surroundings, it was as impressive as if it had been in the best-known temple of the country. The rabbi knew, of course, what was at stake and his address to us and to the bride's family was an emotional mixture of hope and despair. After the wedding, we were given two ration tickets as a wedding banquet and then the waiting began.

It was a long day, lying on the straw-covered floor of the "Schleuse" barrack, waiting for the message that would decide over life or death, at least for the two of us. For the other members of the family, the outcome was already certain. Time went by and the evening came without anything happening. This was a wedding night on the stone floor with hundreds of desperate people squeezed together in a space not much larger than a good-sized living room in an average apartment.

At about four in the morning the wake up call came and cards to the transport were distributed. All three members of my new wife's family received their slips just as expected. Only the two of us did not receive anything, but this by itself did not mean much. Without special permission in writing, nobody was allowed to leave the place. I myself, with my free passage permit, could have probably managed to sneak out, but for her there was no chance. Another wait began.

The transport was summoned to the loading platform and my new in-laws had to leave. There were tears, floods of tears and choking words of love and hope. Finally, the two of us were left alone in the vast entrance hall. We heard the whistle of the engine and the rumbling of the train carrying its 1500 sacrifices for the death of the "great man" Heydrich to the gas chambers of Majdanek.

It was already broad daylight and the cleanup crews began to prepare the Schleuse for the next set of victims. Still nothing. Finally, long after midday, the long-expected message came. It came in the form of two narrow papers: one announcing that my listing in the central evidence had been changed from "single" to "married", and one assigning my wife to a room in the Dresden barracks, where women were accommodated. With these two papers, we could leave the Schleuse, and I brought my new wife to her barracks where the barrack elder assigned her a room and a place on a bunk that, from there on would be her home for more than a year.

STARVATION...

More than 35,000 people died in the Theresienstadt KZ. There were no gas chambers, no mass executions. From what did these people die then? Well, no high-tech killing machine was involved. What the SS used was the oldest, simplest and cheapest method for terminating human life - starvation.

We were not directly starved to death. Young people could survive on the meagre diet of the camp. Not so the older ones. The ghetto diet, barely sufficient in calories, was severely lacking in other essential components. Older people became weaker and weaker by the day and there came a time when they lost hope, and the will to live. They were called "Musselmänner", Mohammedans, at this stage and they knew the end was near. "Hunger typhoid" was the name the doctors gave to the cause of these deaths.

When insufficiently nourished, the body tends to shut down all functions, which are not essential for survival. One of these functions is the drive for the preservation of the species. Women's bodies stop menstruating and men lose interest in the other sex. Exceptions were the small groups of people who could, in one way or another, supplement their regular rations from other sources. "Organizing" was the code word for these activities and they were by no means a safe enterprise. When discovered, "Weisung" was the usual consequence, the euphemism for a death sentence. Kitchen personnel were the most frequent victims.

... AND ILLICIT PLEASURES

This of course did not apply to the well-fed SS guards and the few German civilian employees. They were almost exclusively men and their interest in many pretty Jewish girls around them continued unabated and was kept in check only by fear of Hitler's laws against "Rassenschande", desecration of Aryan blood and honour, with threats of a draconian punishment. However, there is no rule without exception and the following episode can testify to that.

It was after the departure of the German civilian communications officer, Mr. Habicht, that the duties of communications and electrical departments were fused and the German head of the latter, Mr. Bobek (also civilian) was put in charge of the combined unit. Our new boss was a kind person and helped wherever he could. Many survivors of the camp owe their life to his covert assistance.

Mr. Bobek had, after the organizational change, moved his office to the third floor, the former post office building, where most of the telecommunications equipment was installed. Under Mr. Habicht, I had been foreman of a group maintaining and repairing that equipment. Installation and construction of new communication links also belonged to our resort. Most of the facilities involved were of the telephone type and the links were largely bare wires. I have already mentioned how risky for all the members of our group the installation of such a link was.

With Mr. Bobek taking over the group, our duties expanded. Telephone and related services remained our main concern, but when the need arose, and that happened quite often, we had to take care of the electrical supply system as well.

There was a reasonably well equipped workshop for both services installed in the same building. The one for electricity was in the courtyard, the one for communication services on the first floor. Interruptions and other disturbances of that service, once reported, had to be cleared up without any delay. One person had to be on call all the time for any emergencies. Since I was probably the most knowledgeable person of the group, Mr. Bobek insisted that I should be available at all times to back up the person on call in case of a major problem. To carry out these duties I was given a night pass that allowed me to be in the streets after nightfall. I also got a key to the building and had the permission to use it any time of the day or night.

The exchange was staffed by German operators, most of them civilian women. There was supposed to be continuous service, twenty-four hours a day, in the long distance office. But that lasted only a few months. Shortage of personnel forced the abandonment of that regime and the exchange remained without an operator most nights and on weekends. When that happened, it offered us a cherished opportunity. In our workshop, there was a fully equipped bathroom from pre-war times. The water heater still functioned and we took turns soaking in the big tub and lingering in the quietness and relative security of that "extraterrestrial" place. Few places in the camp could provide that feeling.

One Sunday, I decided to enjoy these conveniences. I knew that the operator girl had the day off and, since I was the only one who had a key, I felt pretty safe to be alone in the building. I had a bath and then made myself comfortable on the floor. I had left the door open and heard some noise coming from the upper floor. It was none of my business but I decided to investigate anyway. Walking quietly up the stairs I heard some giggles and some female voices with a lone deep male voice in between. The words I could not discern. I should have been warned by now not to continue further, but I was curious and moved on.

The door to the office complex on the third floor was ajar and as I glanced in, I knew I made a bad mistake. There was our German super boss seated in his office chair, his eyes riveted upon playful Jewish girls in Eve's attire. As I have said, the camp diet and perpetual stress did not support craving for sex and the sight just made me jump back.

It was too late. Mr. Bobek had seen me and shouted:

"What are you doing here?"

I stood there waiting for what would come next.

Then he said, "You have not seen, not heard anything and will not talk ever. Don't ever again show up here, except when on duty. You understand?"

I understood only too well. To do Mr. Bobek justice, he never mentioned what had happened and lent me his support many times when I was in dire straits.

CENSUS

If anything in the ghetto worked well, it was the evidence system. Its task was to keep track, from day to day, of the number of inmates, their names, their places of accommodation, dates of arrival and departure, etc. It appears that the SS command had confidence in that system and its exactness. Whether the episode below was triggered by some special occurrence or whether it was intended just as a random test is hard to say. Anyway, one day it was announced that all inmates, regardless of their work assignment, were to assemble early in the morning on a wide-open space that likely had served in the past for troop marches and parades.

Then it happened. The ghetto had, at that time, some thirty thousand-odd occupants. All inmates had to assemble in the narrow streets of the old town and then march in large units to the assigned locations. Only seriously ill persons in the hospital were spared, along with a few top people of the administration. These were presumably counted separately.

There had been very little time to prepare and organize the event. As was to be expected, confusion reigned paramount. It took many hours until everything was completed and the thirty thousand-odd people arranged in square or rectangular formations. The group to which I belonged had been one of the first to show up. The weather was cool and cloudy and we were all shivering. Of course, no one knew exactly what was afoot and all kinds of rumours continued to swirl around. The mood was not improved by the whole place being surrounded by heavily armed SS troops brandishing their submachine guns and firing a few rounds over our heads from time to time.

Then the counting began. SS men with lists of names wandering through the crowds and crossing out the ones they had encountered. There were mistakes of course, many of them, and when they occurred the procedure started again, from the beginning. Hours went by and the counting had no end. Naturally, no food or water was distributed. To sit down earned a kick from the boot of an SS man or a blow with the butt of the man's submachine gun. Many people could not stand such a long time and simply collapsed, adding only to the overall confusion.

The sun went down and still no end to the counting. Trucks were called in with anti-aircraft searchlights mounted to illuminate the scene and the counting went on. It was close to midnight when the SS gave up. I doubt very much that they had achieved their purpose. Perhaps they had come to the conclusion that the confusion was too large to arrive at exact numbers. Anyway, we were allowed to return to our barrack, more hungry and thirsty than usual, chilled to the bone, but happy to have survived what many of us had expected to take a different and much more serious end.

CAMERAS

In the beginning, the ghetto had a small depot containing small quantities of a few essentials like laundry, shoes, and the like. It was under the administration of the Social Services department, which had the power to distribute, in emergency cases, some of the stored items. After my arrival in the ghetto, I had also been the beneficiary of these services. As time went by, the depot grew and began to contain a wide variety of different items ranging from jewellery to watches, from hearing aids to eyeglasses. These objects originated from a wide variety of sources. These were the belongings of dying persons, if their neighbours did not manage in time to let their most valuable possessions disappear. There was the luggage of persons departed by one of the many outgoing transports, which the owners had to leave behind. And, last but not least, there was the loot of the "lady-birds".

As the size of the depot grew, the SS command turned its attention to it. Much of the clothing it contained was given to the "Winterhilfswerk" (winter assistance), mainly to help protect the inadequately equipped freezing German soldiers at the Eastern front from the cold. Jewellery, items made of gold, including dental prostheses and crowns removed from corpses, were used to bolster the dwindling gold reserves of the Reich, though I suspect that a sizeable portion of that material ended up in the pockets of the SS personnel involved in their administration.

Some rare items that made their way into the depot were photographic cameras, films and other accessories. In the beginning, we disregarded them entirely, with the SS using them for their own purposes. By 1944, when the German defeat became evident even in the ghetto and was considered only a matter of time, cameras and films began to attract interest. Mainly very small cameras that could be hidden under a coat or jacket drew our attention and, in the course of time, we managed to confiscate several of them and hide them in a safe place. They were distributed and put into the hands of a few courageous fellows who, from previous times, had photographic experience. I believe the first photo was made at the unloading of the last transport to arrive in the ghetto.

More and more photos were made in the last days before the SS fled and then more openly and unconcealed after the liberation of the camp. The main restriction was the small amount of film we had available, an amount that under the prevailing conditions at the end of the war could not be replenished. Some of the film I had was spoiled by unsuitable storage, some were ruined by improper development. From perhaps fifty photos I had taken, only less than ten yielded usable pictures. Even these got lost in the turbulence of post war developments.

HEALTH CARE

The healthcare system in the ghetto was fairly well equipped with technology. There was no acute shortage of the most important drugs and other medical supplies. There is no need to say that there were many outstanding physicians among the ghetto population at all times, who were only too happy to work in their profession instead of in a labour commando. However, since physicians were in rich supply, they were expendable and there was a rapid turnover as transports came and went.

The question arises: Why did the SS tolerate and support such a system, that was quite efficient in preserving lives, which later would be destined to die in gas chambers or in front of firing squads? There were likely several reasons. One, but certainly not the most important, was the desire to preserve the largest possible amount of human material for the grinding of the war industry, which suffered a continuous shortage of personnel capable to withstand, at least for several months, the twin pressures of hard manual work and starvation.

Seen from the distorted perspective view of Himmler and company, more important was the desire to use Theresienstadt as a showpiece, where reasonably well equipped and staffed hospitals offered themselves as an outstanding opportunity to show foreign visitors proof of the value Germany placed even on the lives of these subhuman prisoners.

The decisive factor was, in my mind, the almost panicky fear of an epidemic that might break out in the crowded conditions of the camp. That such an epidemic might kill the weakened starved prisoners by the thousands was probably the least of concerns. Rather they feared that such an epidemic might not be confined to the worthless prisoners, but might jump over the walls and abutments and affect the civilian population in the vicinity or even the proud masters from the SS. This view is supported by the emphasis placed upon general hygiene and health services even in pure extermination camps. That fear was not unfounded. When, at the very end of the war, the overall system of the Nazi order was breaking down and with it most efforts of maintaining public hygiene, epidemics of spotty fever and typhoid broke out in many concentration camps and it was almost a miracle that these did not spread to the population at large.

TANGLED WIRES

It was 1944 when the blind hatred of the Nazi regime of anything Jewish went a step further. Up to that time, the Jewish partners of mixed marriages had been spared deportation and the same applied, with some exceptions, to their offspring. Not anymore. The non-Jewish partners in such a marriage were sent to special camps whilst the Jewish ones and so-called half-Jews belonging to the Jewish faith were to be deported to Theresienstadt. To make space for these newcomers, a series of transports east to Auschwitz was organized, each with five thousand persons. Virtually all inmates were to go, with only about 800 to remain to safeguard the essential services of the camp until these could be taken over by the new arrivals. Then they were to follow.

An SS captain, Muess, had arrived in the camp. He was supposed to select the people who were still to remain, at least temporarily. All inmates had to pass in front of him and display their hands. They also had to state their profession. Those with calloused hands who stated their professions as labourers, gardeners or the like, were more likely to stay.

At about the same time, the camp command shuffled its offices. This necessitated a rewiring of the telephone system. A colleague from the electrical department and I were called in to perform the work. The supply situation in Germany had severely deteriorated and there was a shortage of copper. Not even the SS, whose orders usually had the highest priority, could obtain the copper wire, which is generally used for telephone installations. Instead, we had to use the aluminium wire.

This material was extremely brittle. It could not be soldered and connections had to be made by twisting together the wires that were to be connected, or by using screw clamps of which we were given only an insufficient quantity. Either way of interconnection was prone to mechanical failure and required careful manipulation. Electrical properties were also far inferior to copper. We knew that as long as our work was not finished, we were secure from transport, and we worked as slowly as we could without arousing suspicion.

Naturally, the SS kept a watchful eye on us all the time. But all delays could not prevent us from having to report that the work was finished and we were sent back to our barracks. Two or three days later it happened. I received my summons to the next transport, the fourth or fifth in that series. There was little hope in disobeying and so I reported to the transit barracks. By that time, we already had a fairly good idea about what was going on, and so I had with me only a small bag with a few essentials.

At that point, fate intervened. The installation we had just finished exhibited a defect. To our luck it was the special line of the camp commander that had gone dead. A new installation of that kind needs a week or so of test operation, during which faults and mistakes that show up are eliminated. Under pressure from the SS, we had to cut that burn-in period short, but even then we didn't expect serious problems. The SS had undoubtedly counted upon help from the Czech postal service to remove any minor problems that might occur. We had anticipated that and, to make the situation more difficult for them, we had not produced drawings of the system, but I carried all essential information in my head.

Now the camp commander needed urgent instruction from his superiors in Berlin about the schedule and itinerary of the transport, and when he could not use that special line, he summoned, as anticipated, assistance from the post office authorities of the Protectorate. In a hurry, two technicians were dispatched to the camp. Fortunately, they were not overly experienced. They had orders to expedite their work. In addition, they were likely also keen to admire the ancient fortifications again from the outside. Not having any plans, they tried to locate the fault by pulling here and pushing there, a procedure that is not uncommon but spells disaster when used with aluminium wiring. Anyway, in a couple of hours, they managed to disturb everything and the whole system went dead. I do not know what excuse they used when they had to admit that they were not at all able to bring the system back to life.

In the meantime, I was sitting in the "Schleuse", rolling away the time in anticipation of the inevitable. I was shocked and frightened when one of my fellow travellers approached me with the message that the feared and hated SS-Scharführer Heindl had shown up and announced that I should immediately be found and brought to him. I had, of course, no idea the reason for this attention, but knew that being summoned by Heindl did not portend anything good. There was no way out, though; I had to face the music. Another guy came with the same message. He only added that Heindl was getting impatient.

I went through the long cold corridors of the barracks to the main entrance where the sergeant was waiting. I reported to him dutifully in the prescribed way. I was rather flabbergasted when, instead of greeting me with a stream of abuses, he was almost polite. He handed me a paper and asked me to come with him right away. I looked at the paper and saw that it was a pass issued by the commander and authorizing me to leave the transit barracks. It was clear that something important had happened, but I could not even guess what. Of course, you didn't ask questions of Mr. Heindl if you were subhuman and he was master over your life and death. So we went, me always a few steps behind the Scharführer.

From the direction we were going, I gathered that we were heading to the building of the headquarters of the camp command. I concluded that Heindl's visit had something to do with our recent installation, but had no clue as to what for. We were let in without the usual registration at the gate and went up the stairs to the camp commander's office. SS-Obersturmführer Rahm was sitting behind the desk. We had barely closed the door when he jumped up and bellowed at me. "I need to talk urgently with Berlin and the damned fools from the post office have messed things up so much that nothing works anymore in this cursed equipment. You have to fix it and quickly. Tell me what you need."

"I need my tools and instruments."

"Tell me where they are and I will send somebody to bring them."

Now, I was fairly certain that, assuming that I was already halfway on a trip to heaven, the few remaining members of the electrical department had already divvied up amongst themselves everything that I had left behind. Sending an SS man for these things could spell disaster for them and so I objected, "He may not be able to find them. Shouldn't I go myself?"

Rahm shot back, "No way, you stay here. But write down what you need and where to find it."

I had no choice but to comply. Fortunately and to my surprise, nothing had yet disappeared, and the dispatched SS man returned in a few minutes with everything that I had asked him for.

"What now?" Rahm asked.

"Now I have to go to the exchange room."

In the exchange room, the extent of the damage became evident. The aluminium wires were broken in dozens of places, clamps loosened or lost. I was at a loss as to whether the post office workers were simply incompetent or whether they had tried to be saboteurs. Now, I knew that the chances of surviving resettlement in the East were slim. I also knew that the SS were generally more impressed by a bold response than by meekness and submissiveness. All in all, I reasoned, there was not much to lose and I asked Rahm to have a look at the tangle of broken wires and loosened clamps at the terminals of the exchange. "The pass you sent me is for one day only. I have to report back at the transit barracks for the night and there is no way that this can be repaired by then. Furthermore, with this brittle wire material you can expect this to occur again anytime."

Rahm looked at me as if he had guessed my thoughts. "Pass or no pass you will stay here until the work is finished. Then we'll see. But I need to talk to Berlin from my office today. If you can manage that before the evening, you will not regret it."

I knew that was as far as I could expect him to go. Besides, what confidence could I place into an SS man's promise? There was little choice, though. I told him: "If you agree, commander, I can provide you with a temporal before this evening, which will enable you to talk to the outside world. However, restoration of the system will take time and I will need some help. It would be best if it could be the fellow with whom I had worked during the construction."

Rahm nodded consent and Heindl was dispatched to bring him to headquarters. I guess it was quite a shock for him when Heindl appeared at his quarters and dragged him along. I was confident that, by evening, we could manage a temporary connection to meet Rahm's wishes and so we did. The remaining work we saved as much as possible without arousing suspicions. We had already developed some experience in that "good but slow" approach.

We thus managed to delay completion of the work until my transport was gone and even the next one a few days later. Luck had it that this transport was the last one in that series. The rapid advance of the Red Army prevented further transports later on so we had no chance to test Rahm's half promise.

INTRIGUE

A KZ environment has its own morale, ethics and set of values. Theresienstadt was no exception to this general rule. For example, stealing, known commonly in German as "schleusen" (to sneak through or smuggle), from the camp's public stores was not regarded as unethical, but stealing from a fellow prisoner was, and the perpetrators were ostracized and whenever possible, clandestine punishment was meted out. Intrigue and anger between fellow prisoners belonged in the same category. Here is an example of such an intrigue, which concerned me.

At that time, I had been working as foreman of the communications group for about a year. We had built and installed many miles of open wire lines and the telephone system of the ghetto and the SS command was virtually completed. The emphasis of my work had shifted from outdoor construction to indoor maintenance of the exchange mechanism. The experience I had acquired during my time at Prague had served me well and Mr. Habicht from the German post administration had been very content to let me handle almost all work, whilst he took care only of reports, accounting and other administrative duties. In return, he had reclaimed me as indispensable from several transports to which I had been assigned.

Nothing lasts forever, though. The German military machine demanded more and more manpower and staffing was, at civilian organizations, reduced to the bare minimum and below. Consequently, Mr. Habicht was transferred to another position outside the ghetto. As a result, I became suddenly masterless. I had no boss to give me orders but also nobody to shelter me in case of an emergency.

It was during that period that somebody high up in the Jewish administration assigned a new member to our work team as my deputy. To get an assignment to one of the better work outfits commonly required some patronage. Assignment to a unit like ours was a plum, and in the present situation could come only from somebody at the very top of the central bureaucracy. There were a few unusual features in the way this patronage was arranged but, at that time, we did not really worry about that. The newcomer was a middle-aged mechanical engineer with (allegedly) a wealth of industrial experience. That he did not have the faintest knowledge about electrical devices in general and communication equipment in particular did not seem to worry his sponsor. It worried my teammates and me however, because we could not get any help from him in our everyday chores.

Up to now, I had felt reasonably secure. Though I had been put into transports several times, a simple phone call from my boss had always sufficed to get me (and my ghetto wife) out. I knew that with the boss gone the situation would be more precarious. My apprehension turned out to be justified. At the next transport, I was called up. The direction of the group was to be taken over by our recent arrival. There was not much I could do about that and so I packed some belongings into a suitcase I had received from Social Services and made my way to the transit barracks in anticipation of an unknown future full of threats and menaces.

Again, fate decided otherwise. On my way to the "Schleuse" I met Mr. Rust, the Jewish head of the Electrical Services department and my boss in our first workdays in the ghetto. Seeing the suitcase I was carrying he asked, "Why are you going to the "Schleuse"? Have you got a summons?"

When I answered in the affirmative, he became agitated.

"Such a dirty trick! You go back to your lodging and let me handle that. They might not have told you, but since yesterday, you and your people belong to the Electrical Services department. The Reichspost will not send a special official to the ghetto anymore, so his duties and responsibilities are taken over by Mr. Bobek. He is now your boss and since I am his Jewish deputy, you are also my subordinate. It has been agreed by the administration, that any deportation of a worker of our group must in advance be consulted with Mr. Bobek and approved by him. The camp commander has approved that arrangement. Your name was definitely not on the list we went through yesterday. Somebody is playing a dirty game but I will find out who. I am glad we met. If somebody comes and wants to take you to the transport, you don't move before you have heard from me. But I am sure everything will work out fine."

With this, he sped away and I returned to my barracks where I deposited the suitcase. Instead of waiting there for further developments, I went to our group's workshop. When I entered, the boys stared at me as if I was an apparition from the other world. My designated successor had already occupied my workspace and usurped the few things I had left behind. His disappointment over my unexpected return was rather obvious. His greeting was outright hostile. "What are you doing here? You are supposed to be in the "Schleuse" by now. You are bringing misfortune to all of us by disobeying the summons. It came straight from the camp commander. I have to call the ghetto police."

His unusual sharp reaction made me apprehensive. Minor, disregarded episodes from the previous weeks flashed back to my mind. I managed to stay calm and only retorted briefly: "Please go ahead and do what you have to do."

He tried to send one of my boys to call the police but they both refused and he had to go himself. At this point, I decided to play it safe and to return to my barracks as Rust had suggested. Nobody came after me to that place.

I spent the night on my cot, but could not sleep. I knew that the transport was scheduled to leave in the early hours of the morning. Nothing happened and so I went at the usual hour to the exchange office. There I found a message that my successor and I should go up to the former office of Mr.

Habicht and wait there. We did not exchange many words during the several hours we had to wait. Finally, Mr. Bobek, followed by Mr. Rust, appeared. Mr. Bobek addressed us briefly saying,

"The telecommunications group has ceased to exist. Its work will be taken over by the Electrical Services department. Mr. Rust will give you instructions and you will report to him. All workers of the telephone commando belong from now on to the Electrical Services group. The existing foreman will remain in his position. Mr. X," he mentioned the name of my would-be successor "is released immediately. You report to the labour office and ask for a new assignment. Now go."

The mrn in my group were jubilant. They embraced and hugged me as if they themselves had been the intended victims. Piece by piece I learned the story.

The wife of Mr. X, an attractive young woman, had become the secretary of a top man in the administration after her arrival. Eventually, an affair had developed between them. She had somehow found out that I was on the list of essential personnel and had thus a degree of protection from transport. She then convinced her lover, that the best way to safeguard the continuation of their relationship would be to appoint her husband as my successor. Before this could happen, I had to be removed. Her plan was well thought out and would certainly have succeeded. Two events made the plan fail - the decision to make telephone and power services one unit and putting Mr. Bobek in charge of the combined outfit. It was even more important that I was fortunate enough to meet Mr. Rust at just the right moment.

Mr. X and his wife went with the next transport to the East. I do not know whether they had "Weisung" or not. I never heard of them again. They very likely perished somewhere in the East. Her lover remained in his position for another year or so until the SS command decided that the top administrative people knew too much and had to be replaced. The former ones were sent to the East with the remark, "Return undesirable", the SS euphemism for a death sentence. None of them returned. During the three and a half years the ghetto existed, such renewals of the top administrative staff occurred several times and most of these people knew that they were living on borrowed time.

BULLYING

An automatic telephone exchange needs sizeable amounts of electrical power for its operation. That power is generally supplied by big rechargeable storage batteries similar to the batteries in your car. They are filled with diluted sulphuric acid. Whilst the acid largely remains and only rarely has to be replenished, the water evaporates and fresh water has to be added regularly. Of course, tap water cannot be used for that purpose. Instead, distilled water must be used if the batteries are not to be harmed. That replacement water was not available in the ghetto. It was shipped by rail in big glass containers about fifty litres each.

In those early days of the ghetto, there was no regular rail connection. The nearest railway station was in Bohuslavice, about five kilometres away. The arriving transports disembarked there and inmates were marched on foot to the camp. Most equipment, and supplies coming by rail were unloaded there as well, and had to be moved in one way or another to their destination. Our supply of distilled water also was unloaded there. It was then loaded onto a pushcart and brought to the ghetto.

One nice day, I was sent with another man to pick up two demijohns of distilled water at the railway station and bring them back to the camp. At the same time, two empty demijohns were to be delivered to the station, where arrangements had already been made to have them returned to the supply dump of the German Post. We had a four-wheeled cart for these jobs. To protect the glass containers, they were cushioned on all sides by layers of straw taken from the shop where our straw mattresses were stuffed. We got a pass permitting us to leave the camp. We were to have a guard to accompany us all the way. Since no guard was available, our boss accompanied us to the gate to make sure that we could pass. From there we continued by ourselves, Mr. Habicht assumed that the same gendarme would be on duty when we returned. He had not taken the new commander of the Czech gendarmes[12] into account.

For whatever reasons, this man wanted to demonstrate to the SS that he shared their hatred of everything Jewish and that they could rely on him being as mean as they. He had been inspecting the guard at the different exit points and chance had it that he was at the Bohuslavice gate, just when we

---

[12] Captain Theodor Janetschek, a rabid anti-Semite, whose cruelty to inmates surpassed that of the SS.

returned with our cargo.

The gendarme on duty recognized us and wanted to wave us through. He was probably as astonished as we were when his captain reacted with a flood of curses and abuses directed at him as much at us. After studying our passes word by word, comparing dates and checking signatures he started to inspect our cart. We had to lift the filled demijohns from their straw beddings. They were too heavy for us to lift by ourselves and in order to prevent breakage, he ordered his man to help us lift them and even pretended to lend a hand himself. When the cart was empty, he turned it over and we were ordered to pick the straw from the dust and reload the cart. During that work, we were treated to numerous kicks from his jackboots, mainly when we bent down. When the cart was full, he turned it over and we had to start again. The procedure was repeated a third time when we had to pick up each blade of straw separately. When he was satisfied that no single blade was left, we were allowed to reload our water containers. With a kick in the groin and some slaps to the face, we were sent on our return journey. Later we heard that we had been lucky to get away so easily, without serious injury.

DUMPLING

The cots in the ghetto were paired three-level bunks with two persons at each level. For some time I shared the uppermost level with E. T. who was working in the transport commando of the supply group and we became, and still are, good friends. He was later deported to Auschwitz but was one of the lucky ones who survived that death factory.

One of the jobs of his group was to carry heavy sacks of flour up a flight of stairs to the storage magazine of the bakery and empty them there. It was heavy, backbreaking work. The empty sacks were reused. The handlers had the privilege of knocking the empty sacks out and could keep any remainder of flour they could collect. They could not obtain very much that way, but under ghetto conditions, it was a treasure. I did not have such an advantage; but I had an electrical hot plate and, more important, as a member of the electrical group I had a semi-official license to use it.

One of the first days of our being neighbours, E. T. brought the bounty of the day's work, a paper bag with about a quarter pound of flour in it, and we set out to convert that treasure into what we hoped would be a tasty supplement to our regular ration. Neither of us had any experience in cooking or baking. Nor did we have any of the usual ingredients, not even salt. All we had was that dash of flour, a bit of margarine and water.

With great enthusiasm, we started to mix flour and water in a canteen cup to a thick pap, trying to produce something that might become a dumpling. We had added too much water, though, and the resulting mash did not hold together. To amend that, we wrapped the whole thing into a piece of white cloth and put it into boiling water in a canteen cup on the hot plate. That seemed to work fine. However, after a short while we smelled something like burning cloth. Since there was nothing around which might cause that smell but our hot plate, we inspected the latter only to find that the wrapping cloth, which was to hold our dumpling together, had set to the bottom of the cup and been charred. Our precious flour had spread as a runny dough and become a kind of thick soup.

There was nothing more to do to save the day. The soup had no taste at all besides a slight fragrance of burnt fabric, but to pour it away would have been a terrible waste. Therefore, we continued the boil until we thought the flour mush was done, divided it carefully into two equal helpings and finished it off until not a trace was left. The meal was not tasty at all even for our unspoiled palates, but it filled our stomachs and for once, we did not go to bed hungry. It had been a learning experience and next time we would do it better.

INTO THE FIRE

The year 1944 was coming to an end. The armies of the Western Allies had broken out of their Normandy bridgehead and were advancing toward Germany's heartland. From the East, Soviet troops were launching massive attacks that forced the opposing German units into a slowly yielding defence. Theresienstadt was still far from the front line. However, that did not prevent the German High Command from taking precautions in case of a deep breakthrough by the Soviet army. A chain of fortified positions was to be built as defence against that possibility.

Some elements of that chain were located not too far from the ghetto camp. The actual construction was performed by forced labour under heavy guard by SS troops. We had no contact with them and did not know where they came from, whether they were inmates of other concentration camps, Russian prisoners of war or political detainees.

One day our work commando was ordered to assist with the installation of electrical wiring. A truck brought us to the construction site early in the morning and was supposed to pick us up at nightfall. However, when we arrived we found that work had not yet advanced sufficiently to permit wiring to be installed. We were given shovels and mattocks and sent to help dig trenches.

At that time, the Allied Air Force enjoyed absolute supremacy and its fighter-bombers were freely roaming the German skies without any resistance from the Luftwaffe. As a result, during daylight, all road and rail traffic had come to a complete halt. At daybreak, a column of army trucks with fuel for the panzers had sought cover in a small grove, perhaps one thousand feet in front of the place where we were digging. They were camouflaged and sheltered by trees, but that did not prevent a sharp-eyed observer in one of these low-flying planes to discover them.

In a short while, half a dozen planes were overhead, striking the parked vehicles with their cannons and attacking them with bombs. It did not take long and the cisterns were punctured and fuel was flowing out in streams. Seconds later that river of fuel was ignited and a broad front of flames was rapidly advancing towards the trenches where we were labouring. People panicked and tried to flee from the flames. But in that moment the guards, who had been in position at the rear, opened fire with their machine guns and automatic rifles and the people trying to flee fell one after another in a bloody heap. Meanwhile, the flames were coming closer and closer. This left me with two equally unpleasant alternatives: face the bullets of the SS or the advancing flames. Either choice appeared to spell certain death with the difference only in the way death would come.

Perhaps on impulse and in a second, I decided to crawl forward toward the approaching fire. That decision saved my life.

After some 150 feet of crawling, head down and body snuggled tightly to the ground and machine gun bullets flying overhead, I came to a little pond or rather a large puddle. I slipped into the water, which happened to be deeper than expected, and submerged my body as much as I could. The fire came nearer and nearer, but it was not spread any further by the burning fuel oil, just the shrubs and trees ignited by the intense heat.

Then the fire reached the pond where I was hiding. I pressed myself to the bottom with my head under the water and stayed there as long as I could. When I could not hold my breath anymore and put my head out of the water, the front of the fire had jumped across the pond and was eating its way towards the trenches we had been digging. On the side from where the fire had come, only glowing embers were left. The heat was still intense, but I could still breathe some gulps and then hid again underwater. I do not know how long it lasted, but it seemed an eternity.

After a long, long wait, I left my watery hiding place and made my way slowly back to the place where I had come from. It was empty, the SS gone, only dead and dying bodies strewn all over the place. I could have easily fled because I was certainly thought to be dead, but how far could I get in my soaking wet outfit with the yellow star, without food, without money, without outside help? I decided to wait. I reasoned that the incident might not be known in the ghetto and the truck would arrive, as arranged, at dusk to bring us back. It came, but I was the only passenger on that trip. Everybody else had fallen victim to the flames or to the bullets of the SS.

BY THE SKIN OF THEIR TEETH

FIFTEEN HUNDRED LIVES

By February 1945, the war was still raging on, even though the signs of the collapse of German armed resistance were written on the wall. They were visible to most, but not everybody was able to read and interpret them correctly, especially the starved, wretched sub-humans with the yellow star of racial distinction, locked in behind the high walls of the old fortress. Rumours were coming and going, covering the wide range between the wildly exaggerated optimism and despairing pessimism. Whom to believe, that was the question.

It was against that backdrop that the SS command, one beautiful morning, announced via the Council of Elders, that a new transport of 1200 persons was to be assembled. That in itself was not new. Too many similar announcements (or more realistically, orders) had already been issued before and under the soft persuasion of the Schmeissers[13], faithfully obeyed. But there was a difference. The destination of these transports had never been given more in detail beyond the terse remark, "to the East". However, the names of the likely destinations were on everybody's mind. The names Auschwitz, Birkenau, Treblinka, and others had been swirling around with the sinister connotation attached to them. Participants in these transports had always been selected partly by the SS command itself with the bulk chosen by the Jewish administration. Participation of the selected persons was enforced by the most severe penalties.

This time it was different. The SS command determined only the total number of transported, and stipulated that only inmates from Germany, Austria, the Netherlands and the Protectorate were to go.

---

[13] Schmeisser, the German submachine gun (Machinenpistole) MP 40, in use 1939-1945.

Another stipulation was that eligible were only inmates who had already spent a certain time in the ghetto. The big difference was that neither the SS command nor the Jewish administration put forward any names. All people who met these criteria were invited to volunteer. The main enticement was its destination: the transport was to go to Switzerland.

Switzerland was the only free island in the sea of occupied Central Europe; it sounded too good to be true. There had been so many broken promises by the SS, so many outright lies spread around, that the news was received with general disbelief. The result was that there were hardly any volunteers. Those who dared to take the plunge were mostly people who had some private relations to one or the other of the few top officials of the self-administration who knew or believed to know and passed that knowledge on to their friends. So people had to be forced to join the transport as it happened so many times before.

When the transport finally left the camp, its composition with regard to countries of origin was quite different from that prescribed by the original instructions. For one reason or another, most of the participants from the Protectorate had been replaced by other nationalities, most of them Dutch. The suspense that prevailed after the train had departed was almost palpable. The camp was abuzz with conflicting news. There was talk of a telegram confirming the arrival of the transport at the Swiss border. Another rumour claimed that the train had been seen crossing the border of the General Government (the former Poland) and heading east.

However, after a few days, post cards began to arrive in the ghetto with Swiss stamps on them, with the handwriting of people known to have been in the transport. Even that did not allay all doubts. They vanished only when reports of BBC stations were received by some of the clandestine radio receivers in the ghetto describing the arrival of the transport in Basel, Switzerland, and even broadcasting fragments of interviews with the arrivals. Many an inmate of the group that had been eligible for participation in the Swiss transport regretted that he had not volunteered. Now, it was too late and nothing could be done.

Of course, the SS high command had not agreed to that transport for nothing. Speculations about the reasons were ripe. Some people claimed to know that the price was the return of German civilian prisoners. Others claimed that it was a big ransom paid personally to Heinrich Himmler, Reichsführer SS and the commander of all German police and security forces. Adherents of the latter theory claimed that until more money was collected, further transports would follow. Who was right I cannot say. After all, there might have still been other reasons involved, perhaps of a more political nature. I was rather skeptical about further follow-up transports.

For the next several weeks nothing happened. Rumours (largely confirmed after the war) began to fly around that some high ranking officials of the extreme radical wing of NSDAP, among them Ernst Kaltenbrunner, the head of the Reich Security Head Office (RSHA), and Joachim Ribbentrop, the minister of foreign affairs, had intervened with Hitler and got him to block any future attempts to use Jews as bargaining chips for whatever purpose. Some of the activities of the SS at that time, for which it was difficult to find a rational explanation, lent credence to these rumours.

A picture from the quarantine camp in St. Gallen.
(Photo: Stadtarchiv (Vadiana) St. Gallen, courtesy of USHMM Photo Archives.)

Nevertheless, to the surprise of most (me included,) in late March the SS announced that a second transport, this time of 1500 people, was to be assembled with the destination Switzerland. Participation was supposed to be mandatory for all so-called "Prominents". The Prominents were a designated group of Jewish prisoners from all countries of occupied Europe, who had the misfortune to fall into the hands of the occupying forces, but the names of which were internationally known. Members of that group enjoyed a number of privileges. The most important of these was that they were automatically deported to Theresienstadt and not to one of the many death camps to which their less fortunate compatriots were mostly sent. They also enjoyed protection from the liquidation transports that continually thinned the number of inmates of the ghetto. There were also a number of minor privileges that were less important for survival, but made day to day life in the camp more tolerable.

The number of Prominents in the ghetto was not sufficient to fill up the transport. Therefore, it was graciously announced that volunteers would be accepted until the full number was reached. This time only the inveterate disbelievers mistrusted the announcement and there was no shortage of volunteers. Long lines formed at the registration station and people were even fighting among themselves for a place in the queue.

I was in a quandary. Even from our restricted information it was clear that the war was about to end soon. How soon, that was the question. At the same time, I knew about some highly suspicious things going on in the ghetto. The idea of being able to weather the last months of the war in the safety of Switzerland was almost overpowering. On the other hand, I had witnessed too many lies and dirty tricks by the SS to have much confidence in their promises. Even more important, I knew that the son of Dr. Murmelstein had retracted his original application to join the transport. Dr. Murmelstein was chairman of the Council of Elders, i.e. head of the ghetto administration, and known to be in good relations with the SS commander of the camp, SS-Obersturmführer (First Lieutenant) Karl Rahm. His son bowing out of the transport only reinforced my distrust and I decided not to register for it. It was not long before my suspicions were confirmed.

My ghetto job at that time was maintenance and repairman for everything that had to do with electricity. Telephones use electricity and, therefore, belonged to my domain. That had two advantages: I had relative freedom of movement inside the ghetto and occasionally even outside. Then I was under the watchful eye of a Czech gendarme who was fortunately blissfully ignorant about what I was supposed to do. Standard equipment for my job was a case of special tools, climbing irons to climb up telephone poles and a set of spare parts. The stuff was heavy but I carried it with me even when I did not expect to need it. It came in handy for purposes other than simple repair work, and then it was worth its weight in gold (or in cigarettes, which was the common ghetto currency). One of these tools was a special earphone that let you listen to a phone line without disturbing an ongoing conversation. It was used a lot, though predominantly for purposes which were fundamentally different from what my guardian angel imagined. Although I could never listen for any length of time, the fractions of information that I gathered were frequently sufficient to give me a good idea of things afoot.

Fate allowed that, by sheer accident, I stumbled upon a telephone conversation between the commander of the camp and the Jewish elder Murmelstein. Shortly before rumours had circulated that Paul Dunant, Swiss delegate of the International Committee of the Red Cross from Geneva, Switzerland, was to visit the ghetto. There had been visits of the Red Cross before and usually some temporary improvements had preceded them. However, these quickly vanished once the visitors were gone. In that conversation I fortuitously overheard how Rahm ordered Murmelstein to prevent, at all costs, the Swiss visitors from learning about the planned new transport to their country.

Understandably, my already lingering suspicion became almost certainty that something terrible was afoot. What could be the reason for the SS boss wishing to conceal, at all cost, the Swiss delegate from learning of the departure of a train of human barter material to Switzerland? That the Germans had one of their dirty tricks up their sleeve was clear in my mind. And that the lives of many of my fellow prisoners were at stake appeared equally obvious.

The immediate question now was what to do, how to counter the SS treachery without committing outright suicide and, on top of that, endangering the lives of others. It was obviously necessary to pass the message on to Dunant, hoping that he might be able to cross the intentions of the SS in a way that would not provoke them to desperate retribution. We knew that Germany was losing the war, although we could only guess the details. Anyway, I surmised that international public opinion, which only a year ago would have carried zero weight with the SS, might now be able to sway at least the less fanatic elements amongst them or those realistic enough to be concerned about their own safety after the anticipated collapse of German resistance. That might give Dunant the necessary leverage that he did not have at previous occasions.

The question was how to approach him or the other member of the delegation.[14] Obviously, that was not possible overtly. It was certain that Dunant and Lehner would be strictly guarded and that few, if any, non-SS persons would be allowed access to them. It also seemed very likely that hidden microphones might monitor every word spoken in their company. It was obvious that I would not belong to the few people given the opportunity to talk to him.

Then there was the question: who would believe me based on a few overheard words that could have been misinterpreted? Who would stake his life upon such a shaky belief?

Hope is a strong believer. You hope against despair, against your own reason, against the many negative experiences with German promises and assurances that in the final event turn to crude and cruel deceptions. With whom to consult in that matter? Whom to trust that would not go to the SS and turn you in for the promise of a few privileges?

I spent many a sleepless night pondering my options. The easiest one was not to do anything, to ignore that ominous order, and forget it had ever been issued. It was the easiest one and least dangerous. There were no witnesses and I was not assigned to the transport. Just because it was so easy and cowardly, I ruled this option out almost the moment it came to mind. Mind you, there is not much heroism left in a person after years of imprisonment and deprivation. Its place is

---

[14] Dr. Otto Lehner, who wrote an enthusiastic report on the conditions in which the Jews were living in Terezín.(Holocaust.cz)

taken by a steadfast desire not to succumb, to put up an inconspicuous but firm and stubborn resistance to the inflicted indignities.

There existed a small but well organized and, of course, clandestine group involved in making plans for resistance, even armed, if there was no alternative left. The group was kept small for security reasons. Another reason was the left-leaning ideology of its leaders, who mostly had been members of the underground Communist Party and still maintained some secret links to that party. Very few people knew about that and it became public knowledge only in May, when Soviet tanks rolled through the camp.

One of the top members of that group was an acquaintance, perhaps even a friend of mine, an engineer named Vogel. It was to him I turned for advice. It was a long discussion, taking the better part of the night. Vogel was, from the beginning, rather distrustful, suspecting a trap set up by the SS and, perhaps out of customary disbelief, because I did not belong to his group. Finally, he became convinced that the deceit I suspected was real and we began looking for solutions. Many were proposed only to be rejected by one argument or the other. Finally, we agreed upon one that appeared to be promising and not involving excessive risks. One of the members of the group of Prominents was a former French Minister of Merchant Marine, Léon Meyer, who was there with his wife and daughter Denise.[15] I had occasionally helped them with minor services and repair work, and Denise and I had become good friends. From her I had learned that Paul Dunant had been a good friend of the family and we had reasons to assume that Dunant, knowing that Meyer, his wife and daughter were interned in Theresienstadt, would certainly express the wish to see him, a wish that the SS would find difficult to refuse.

The discussion would very likely be in German, in which Dunant and Meyer were fluent, but a few words interspersed in French would not arouse much suspicion. We were betting on the probability that the SS guard that would be present would understand French poorly or not at all. It could be expected that a few words in French in a

---

[15] Léon Meyer and his family were transferred to Theresienstadt from Bergen-Belsen KZ.

conversation largely in German would escape his attention. It was the message about the planned transport, ostensibly to Switzerland; Meyer would pass to Dunant in French. There was certainly a risk involved and the question was whether Meyer would be prepared to assume the risk. In the relatively sheltered position he was in, he might feel that he personally was in no imminent danger and might believe that our story was just a fabrication. The only way out seemed to be to talk to him and to explain everything in person. Even then, success was far from certain.

Much as we tortured our brains, no better plan came to our minds. After almost a night long discussion, we came to the conclusion that the only feasible way was via Meyer's daughter Denise. I knew her well enough to be able to talk to her openly. It was clear that we could not meet in public. However, as an electrical maintenance man I had easy access to their accommodation where we could talk undisturbed without the danger of being overheard. In this context, I should remark that one of the privileges of being a Prominent was accommodation in a semi-private room together with your family. There was no problem in carrying out that plan. Denise had a quick, sharp mind. She also had enough confidence in me to trust my words without much effort to persuade her, and she was soon convinced.

With her father, it was not that easy. During his long political career, the old gentleman had learned to be skeptical and to discount fifty percent and more of everything presented to him. His first question, sometimes proffered aloud, sometimes silently to himself, was, "To whose advantage is it?" The question became especially urgent in the present case. The suspicion we presented to him shook his silent trust in the sincerity of the Germans, who had always treated him politely, if not with respect. There beckoned the hope that in a few days his deprivations would be over and the news I brought was threatening to shatter that hope. At least he listened, and listened for hours at a time.

He was well aware that the dilemma he was facing was not a hypothetical one. He and Denise were supposed to go with the transport and the Germans had suggested that he would be in charge of any discussions and negotiations with the Swiss authorities. Now all those promises were to come to nothing. Yes, he expected to meet Dunant, the Germans had already hinted that and warned him not to talk about anything beyond personal matters. Allegedly, he could thereby jeopardize delicate negotiations at the international level.

The conversation swayed back and forth, but finally I prevailed with the support of Denise, who had significantly less confidence in the sincerity of the SS than her father. As expected, the conversation between Meyer and Dunant was to take place in German. Of course, the main purpose was to make it easier for the listening SS man to understand and follow the conversation. The suggestion was that Meyer would try to bring the message across through a few words in French, inserted into the general flow of conversation, purposely led in somewhat stumbling German.

The plan worked beyond expectations. Of course, I was not present at the meeting of the two and in the way things developed afterwards, it appeared unwise to seek contact with the Meyers in the weeks and months to come.

Dunant kept his inspection routine, visiting the hospital, some of the kitchens, even some of the barracks.[16] On the day of his departure, Rahm, the camp commander, called an unprecedented public meeting of the inmates in a small square behind one of the barracks. There was a small podium where he and Paul Dunant were standing, facing the crowd of prisoners. Whether Rahm gave a speech, I do not remember. Anyway, nobody would have paid much attention because the credibility of the SS was well below zero. However, the words of Dunant still sound in my ears, half a century after they were spoken.

"The war is coming to an end and freedom is again awaiting you. Remain prudent and courageous and don't lose hope." When he had finished his brief address, he abruptly turned to the SS officer standing at his side and said, "Herr Obersturmführer, why do I have no knowledge about that new transport to Switzerland, which is supposed to leave in a few days?" The SS man was flabbergasted. That question was certainly not what he had expected. Before he had

---

[16] The Red Cross delegation arrived on 6 April 1945.

collected his wits and came up with a credible reply, the Swiss man threw the gloves to the floor in front of the feet of the SS commander. Without a further word, he went to his car waiting a few feet away and drove away.

We all expected something to happen, at least an outburst of rage or threats, but nothing of that kind occurred. Rahm, though visibly shaken and pale, stepped down from the podium as if nothing had happened and ordered the Czech guards, the gendarmes, to disperse the crowd in a hurry.[17]

The next day it was announced that the transport to Switzerland was cancelled. After the war when the SS had fled, we found documents that indicated that the train carrying the transport was to be attacked by German planes and SS troops at the border to Bavaria and all passengers were to be killed in the attack. The blame was then to be given to the "boiler makers"[18], the name given to the Allied low-flying fighter-bombers, which at that time roamed freely and almost without opposition, over most of the skies of Germany.

After the war, I tried to meet Mr. Meyer, who had been the mayor of Le Havre[19] in France before the war. Political events in Central Europe did not allow that and I never had a chance to see him again. And Denise, if she is still alive, is supposed to live in the United States, but where and under which name, I was never able to find out.

---

[17] Another risky act against this transport was a speech of Dr. Murmelstein to the delegates, in which he twice said, "Das Schiksal Theresienstadts bereitet mir Sorgen." The delegates then visited SS-Gruppenführer Frank, the Reichsminister for the Protectorate, who promised that there would be no further transports. (http://www.czmpm.com/teresin.html)

---

[18] "Boiler makers" attacked mainly locomotives whose boilers they perforated by strafing to put them out of operation.

---

[19] Meyer was the mayor of Le Havre between December 1919 and June 1940, not after the war.

BETWEEN HIMMLER AND GÖRING

In the First World War, Reichsmarschal (Marshal of the Empire) Hermann Göring had served as a pilot in the wing commanded by the German fighter ace, "The Red Baron", Manfred von Richthofen. It was at least partly on these grounds that he advanced in the Third Reich to be commander in chief of the German Luftwaffe (air force). His observer and navigator during the last part of his career in Richhofen's squadron was a Jewish flyer. I'll call him here Mr. Z.

When peace finally came in 1918, the careers of the two men separated, but they remained in contact with one another. After all, they had gone through many life and death situations together. An error in judgement, a mistake of either one could have cost the lives of both. That a close bond was formed between them was only natural. When Hitler rose to power and the persecution of Jews began to gain momentum, Göring, his second in command, used his position to bestow upon his former comrade in arms the title of "honorary Aryan". This sheltered Mr. Z for many years from the anti-Jewish discrimination measures of the regime and enabled him to lead a normal life, like any other German civilian.

This was not to the liking of some of the fanatics surrounding Himmler, the "Reichsführer" (supreme leader) of the SS, who was for much of the time the principal competitor to Göring in Nazi hierarchy. For a long time, Göring was too powerful for anybody, even Himmler, to challenge openly. But in mid 1945 when the defeat of the Luftwaffe had weakened Göring's position and, maybe, that he had somewhat fallen out of favour with Hitler, still the supreme boss. Himmler or somebody in Hitler's entourage made a decision. The "honorary Aryan" was picked up in the middle of the night by the Gestapo. After being held for a few days in some obscure place incommunicado, he was deported to Theresienstadt.

Probably in order not to antagonize Göring, he was given the status of a "prominent person" and protected from further transports. I have no doubt that Göring learned about the fate of his former comrade in arms. He was either powerless to do something about it or did not think him worth entering into an open conflict with Himmler and his all-powerful SS camarilla.

Whatever the reason, Mr. Z remained in Theresienstadt until the end of the war. I know that he returned to his old hometown in Germany, never to be heard from again.

The smouldering conflict between the two most powerful of Hitler's deputies is also illustrated by the following episode:

The invention of radar and the successful rise of that device then unknown to the Germans contributed very much to the failure of the "Blitzkrieg", a lightning-fast war of the Luftwaffe against England after the fall of France. The initially big and heavy device was gradually perfected and reduced in size and weight until it could be mounted into an aeroplane and used in aerial combat. I believe it was in early 1943 when a British plane equipped with radar was shot down over Rotterdam in Holland.[20] The self-destruct features built into the device that should have prevented it falling into enemy hands failed to operate. The Germans sifting through the debris of the plane got hold of it. It was with little damage. A large-scale effort immediately began to examine the device, to analyse its design and to copy it so that it could be reproduced in Germany. Time was of the essence.

To hasten the process, all scientific and technical manpower that could be spared from other projects was put to work. Among the inmates of the ghetto were, at that time, two outstanding experts of international reputation, Drs. G. and K. Somebody involved in the investigation of the Rotterdam device must have made the Luftwaffe command aware of their presence in Theresienstadt. It is probable that the matter was even brought to the attention of Göring himself. He must have been anxious to learn about the secrets of airborne radar, which had given the Allied Air Force a tremendous advantage over their Luftwaffe counterparts. It is likely that he personally approved of the plan to exploit talents of the Jewish scientists by putting them to work in a German research facility amongst German scientists.

Whatever the background, Drs. G. and K. were summoned one day to the camp command. They were told that they were to be released from the ghetto and transferred to Berlin, where they should work on projects of high

---

[20] Stirling Pathfinder, carrying the H2S radar set, was shot down over Rotterdam on a raid to Cologne on 2/3 February 1943.

priority, in the setting of a research institute. They were to leave in the next few days. In the meantime, they were given new civilian clothes without the telltale yellow star. A couple of days later, accompanied by an SS officer in plain clothes they boarded a first class train compartment in the regular express train to Berlin, and that was the last we knew of them.

Only after the war, we learned that upon arrival in Berlin, they were received by SS guards from the concentration camp Gross-Rosen. Instead of the Luftwaffe research institute, where they were supposed to have been transferred, they were brought to the latter camp. They survived the war there. Dr. K. moved to some place overseas and I have never heard of him since. Dr. G. returned to Prague where he became technical director of an important research institute. After the communist takeover of Czechoslovakia he allegedly committed suicide by jumping out the window of his apartment. Those who knew him well are convinced that it was not suicide but murder, though the motives are, at least to me, unclear to this day.

LAST MINUTE SALVATION

The following episode was told to me by an old lady, formerly in the ghetto and living now in Prague. I have little reason to doubt the truth of her story.

"My transport from Theresienstadt landed us in Auschwitz. I was lucky enough to pass Dr. Mengele's deadly scrutiny and survive. However, my stay in Auschwitz was short and marked only the beginning of a journey through one recreation camp of the SS after another with Bergen-Belsen being the last station.

In early 1945, when the Allied armies had crossed the Rhine and were approaching the camp, the SS decided to evacuate the camp and to send the inmates on one of the infamous death marches. Just at that time, I was down with a bout of spotty fever and in bed in the sickroom. Spotty fever, being strongly contagious, meant I was prohibited from leaving the chamber. Sickness and hunger had weakened me to the extent that I could hardly stand on my feet, let alone walk any distance. By the perverse logic of the SS, I was considered unfit for evacuation and remained in the camp, together with some other seriously ill prisoners and some sanitary and service personnel.

However, the reprieve did not last long. A couple of weeks later, the Allied armies had come too close for the liking of our "guardian angels." Therefore, they decided that complete liquidation of the camp and the remaining inmates would be the easiest solution to the problem. Early one morning, all of us left were marched into the courtyard. Those who could not walk even the smallest distance were encouraged with some boot kicks and rifle butt punches and in the worst cases were carried out by the few of us who were healthy and strong enough. There we stood under the clear morning sun shivering and trembling in the cool air. The courtyard was surrounded by grim looking guards and, here and there, the snout of a machine gun could be seen between them. To our rescue came the German thoroughness. We were counted and counted again and somehow the numbers did not match their files.

Hours went by, the sun was already high and its rays warmed us pleasantly in our threadbare nightgowns, and we heard the rumble of heavy engines. At first, we thought that it was coming from airplanes, that we had so often heard overhead on their way to the bombardment of targets in the interior. The rumbling came closer, though, and it became clear that it did not come from the skies but from the ground. The SS were listening too, but did not seem to be concerned.

Then the gate sprang open and in its opening appeared the cannon of a tank, a British tank. The tank rolled into the courtyard where we stood arranged for the final solution, followed by a dozen or so others. The SS opened fire on them, but light infantry weapons good enough for killing unarmed prisoners were no match for the armour and cannon of the tanks. The fight lasted only a few minutes until the once so proud and haughty SS men started to run as fast as they could with shells bursting among them and the tanks' machine guns mowing them down.

Later we found out that it was a British armoured unit that had saved us, likely in the last moment. The unit had lost its way in the surrounding woods and when they saw a compound fenced in with barbed wire and guard towers, they had decided to investigate. They had heard the term "concentration camp", but had no clear concept of its meaning. Perhaps they did not even believe in its existence and thought that it was only a fabrication of the propaganda machine. Who knows?

Anyway, when they saw the reality, the emaciated figures with their feet barely supporting them and the bloody corpses among them, felled by the last minute machine gun fire of the SS aimed at us, not at them, they began to believe. That they were shocked by what they saw is definitely an understatement.

There is no doubt that their timely appearance had saved our lives, but their desire to help also claimed its victims. The soldiers offered their rations, their chocolate and other goodies that they had in abundance, and who would blame the starved skeletons who devoured these presents as if there was no tomorrow? And for many of them there wasn't. After years of starvation and months of sickness, their stomachs were not able to accept the sudden offerings. Severe stomach cramps were the consequence for many and for the weakened bodies they were the final straw. Later, when a Red Cross unit arrived, a careful dietary regime was installed to bring us back to strength. But for many it was already too late."

WHEN HELL WAS OVER

BOOBY TRAP

The Allied forces knew that the Main Fortress of Terezín served as an internment camp and the Small Fortress as something even worse. That's why it was spared attacks by the Allied Air Force, large groups of which we were used to seeing, in the last months, flying overhead to some unknown destination. The Germans had found that out as well and had moved the archives of the Reichssicherheitshauptamt (RSHA), the principal intelligence office of the SS, to the camp.[21] They assumed correctly that this location would save that highly sensitive installation from air attacks.

However, when the armoured columns of the Soviet army moved in disagreeably close, preservation became less important. Preventing the documents stored in the archives of RSHA from being discovered became the first priority. A small amount of the material was likely carted away and hidden. However, it was impossible to move away the bulk of the stored documents and they had to be destroyed. Fires were burning in the courtyard of the buildings for days. Occasionally, the wind carried some pieces of paper away from the pyre. Members of the SS security service could then be seen frantically chasing them. They could not be retrieved and here and there a half-burnt, but still legible, scrap of paper fell into our hands and was immediately hidden away. Most of the paper saved contained the names, code names and other details of foreign collaborators and secret agents of the SS intelligence service. When the Russian intelligence got wind of that material, they were as keen to get their hands on it, as the SS had been to destroy it.

The destruction of the intelligence archives was completed just a day or two before the Russian troops arrived. By then, all the SS personnel had fled

---

[21] Actually, the archives were transferred from Berlin to two barracks and two neighbouring houses already in July 1943.

and the buildings, former barracks, stood empty.

We were, of course, curious to see what was left of what were previously so carefully guarded secrets stored in several big buildings. We could now move freely within the perimeter of the former fortress and the guards at the entrance of some of the barracks were gone. We were still wearing the yellow Star of David, but now with pride to identify us as former inmates. With an older friend of mine, who had also been working in the electrical department, I went to explore the secrets of one now deserted building.

First, we went to the upper floor, where offices and archives had been housed. But inspecting as closely as we could every nook and cranny, we could not find anything of interest. The rows of office chairs, writing desks and storage cabinets were certainly not what our fantasy had expected. No trace of papers, secret documents or photographs. In this respect, the SS had been painstakingly thorough. Disappointed, we went room-to-room, finding nothing noteworthy anywhere. We were about to give up the search when my companion suggested we might have a look at the ground floor.

The ground floor in these old barracks consisted of large vaulted rooms running side by side the whole length of the building. The entrances were closed by heavy doors that led into a covered corridor open to the barrack's yard. In the times of the Empress Maria Theresa, these vaults served as magazines for supplies and weaponry and also as stables for the horses of mounted troops. We went from one room to another only to find that they were locked and we were not strong enough to pry them open. Finally, we came to one that, though locked as well, yielded to our pushes and sprung open.

There were no windows, and in the dim light coming through the door opening, we saw a sea of metal drums of the kind that is used to store movie film. They were scattered in singles or in low stacks all over the floor. Most of them were sealed by strips of fabric, or in some cases by wire wound around them. It seemed that they were reels shot by field reporters of the army and SS. Of course, we wanted to see some of the scenes recorded on the reels but decided to wait until we had time to inspect the place more thoroughly.

Then my eye fell on a large stack of, apparently unsealed, drums piled up near the door. A large piece of metal, looking like the weight of an old-fashioned pendulum clock, was sitting on the top of the pile, seemingly to weigh it down and to prevent it from tilting. A piece of string went through an eyelet at the upper face, with the other end attached to a nail on the wall. The whole contraption looked innocent enough, at least to me (who had no experience in devious military gadgetry). I loosened the end of the string attached to the whole thing and lifted that piece of metal from the stack of containers for inspection. It looked somehow strange, causing me to call my companion who was standing nearby. That call was my luck; otherwise I would not be able to tell you the story.

My colleague had served in the Czechoslovak army and had some experience with mines, booby traps and similar gadgets. With a glance, he grasped the situation. With a quick jump he tore the thing I was still holding out of my hands and hurled it out of the door onto the courtyard. It was just in time, because the thing exploded even before it touched the ground. Fortunately, the courtyard was empty and nobody was hurt. We were both pale and shaken, but unhurt. If the bomb had exploded inside the vault, not only would we have been torn to pieces, but also the films might have caught fire and the whole building would have gone up in flames.

The sound of the explosion brought a Russian army patrol to the place. They came running, guns ready, probably suspecting a raid by some SS stragglers. We got some scolding for having been thoughtless and the whole space was sealed off while army specialists searched for other booby traps. A day or two later, all the films were loaded into an army vehicle and hauled away so we had no opportunity to view any of them. I only heard from Russian officers that some of the materials were recordings of the wholesale slaughter of the Jewish population in the East, of people tortured to death and similar achievements of the Nazi elite.

INFORMATIVE DOCUMENTS

Our search for documents in the former building of the "Reichsicherhertshauptamt" archives had been futile. Therefore, we turned our attention to what, before the war, had been the hotel Viktoria, which during ghetto times had housed the members of the SS command and their offices. To be precise, the staff of the command belonged to the SD,

(Sicherheitsdienst, Security Service), an elite special branch of RSHA, doing intelligence work for SS. Actually, we did not expect to find too much, but were pleasantly surprised in this regard.

At first, we concentrated a lot of our attention upon the office and desk of the SS-Obersturmfürher Rahm, who had been the camp commander during the last year or so. As expected, we did not find anything noteworthy. Rahm had done a good job cleaning out his desk. Fortunately, not everybody had been so thorough. In another room, we found a filing cabinet chock-full of older papers. Nonetheless, these old documents contained a great deal of interesting information. There was a report about the execution of twelve persons by hanging, the alleged crime being contact with the outside world. I had heard about that incident which had occurred before my arrival in the ghetto. We found an order from a higher SS command that in the future, executions or similar affairs were not to be carried out at Theresienstadt. Instead, the prisoners involved were to be sent to camps in the East, some of which were named, accompanied by instructions about the desired further treatment. To us these instructions were known under the name "Weisung".

We found documents referring to the fake exchange transport to Switzerland in early 1945. The papers named the air force units that were to bomb the train at the border to Bavaria and gave the disposition of the land units that were to massacre any survivors. Organization, timing and other details of the ambush had to be worked out with military precision. Also, we found a letter severely reprimanding Rahm for having allowed the Swiss visitors to learn about the fake transport and its composition, mainly with regard to foreign nationals. The letter also contained instruction to find the source of the leak, to arrange for the liquidation of all persons involved and to take all conceivable steps to prevent another similar occurrence.

There was more material of interest and significance found in that room, which obviously had been forgotten or where the person charged with the destruction had been in too much of a rush to save his own life. The most important of all was a fairly recent folder with documents and drawings found in a cabinet in the same room. It showed that, for us, the Red Army had arrived just in time.

The folder contained detailed drawings dealing with the conversion of some of the casemates in the fortress walls to gas chambers. The documents gave instructions on how to operate them. Since the existing crematorium would not have the necessary capacity and an expansion did not appear feasible, various ways of disposing of the bodies were discussed. The numbers considered corresponded to the size of the camp before the steady stream of death marches had begun to arrive, which had swollen the size of the inmate population to many times the one considered in these plans.

We would have loved to keep these papers and we had time to study them. However, when the Soviet command got wind of our finding, it did not take long for a unit of the NKVD (the Soviet intelligence service) to appear, to confiscate everything and to move it away similarly as they had done with the film material mentioned previously.

DRINK TO COMRADE STALIN'S HEALTH!

It was May 1945, during the last days of the war that an endless column of German troops had been rumbling south on the main highway which skirted the perimeter of the ghetto. They were shooting wildly at anything that moved on the roadside, real or imaginary. They were on a desperate flight before the armoured columns of the Red Army which, coming from the north, were pressing towards Prague to save the uprising there from being crushed. It is almost impossible to express in words the enthusiasm with which the Red Army tanks were greeted when they finally arrived.

Squeezed between the Allied armies advancing from the west and the Russians coming from the East, the main SS command had decided to evacuate the concentration camps that were in the path of the advancing enemy armies. The remaining inmates were sent on what came to be known as death marches, because those who were too weak to keep up with the column, who stumbled and fell were treated by the SS guards with a shot to the head. There were many of those who met that fate and died a few days before their suffering would have come to an end.

Years of starvation were not the only reason. Rigidly enforced hygiene had collapsed and epidemics between the inmates were rampant, with typhoid and spotty fever the main killers. Many of these death marches had converged upon Theresienstadt, which was now crammed to the brim with these emaciated souls. There is little doubt that, had the Red Army arrived much later, hygiene would have broken down also here and most of the population of the camp, newcomers and old-timers alike, would have fallen victim to the epidemics.

Maybe that outcome had even been planned by the SS. It did not materialize because of the rapid intervention of the Russian command. The whole camp was declared quarantined and, without written permission of the Russian commanding officer, nobody was allowed to enter or to leave the camp. The Czech Protectorate gendarmes who had already fled were replaced by Russian soldiers who had strict orders to shoot at anybody who would violate that order.

I was assigned, at that time, to the chief physician of the Red Army detachment that had been put in charge of the camp. My duties were maintenance and repair of medical equipment. My boss had in pre-war times been Professor of Medicine at the University of Kiev but had been with the army already since the German invasion of the Soviet Union.

One evening, he invited a colleague and me for supper at his lodging. The meal was ample and, for our starved stomachs, a feast. When the meal was over, an orderly served each of us a fairly large glass filled to the brim with a clear, colourless liquid. Now I knew of the Russian fondness for vodka so I assumed that we had been served that or a similar kind of beverage. Of course, it had been years since my last glass of anything containing alcohol. I also knew that the quantity in the glass, although perhaps perfectly okay for the well-fed Russian soldiers accustomed to that beverage, might have disastrous effects upon our weakened bodies. Before I could do anything, our host rose, glass in hand and said, "Let's drink to the health of our great leader, comrade Stalin. Bottoms up!"

My colleague and I were both hesitant in our response. Of course we rose dutifully, but instead of emptying our glasses we just sipped a little of their content which proved to be rather sharp but tasteless. Now, that half-hearted response infuriated our host. He pulled a pistol out of his holster and pointing its muzzle toward us shouted: "I cannot tolerate such disrespect to our great leader. You empty your glasses or I shoot."

He seemed to be dead serious about that and so we poured the contents of our glasses down. He immediately became his former friendly self again.

"That's better. I hope you liked it. Do you know what you were drinking?"

"Vodka," I ventured in reply.

He began to laugh. "Vodka is for our troops in the field. What you had was pure medical spirit with surface anaesthetic added to take away some of the sharpness."

I don't know what happened later. After several minutes, I passed out and when I came back to my senses I found myself on a cot in a field hospital of the Soviet army. I was told that I had been delivered to them just in time and wondered how I could have become so intoxicated. It would have been a pity to leave this world just at the beginning of a new life and that only because of a toast to the great leader.

CRUEL REVENGE

With Theresienstadt converted to a quarantine station for more than 50,000 former prisoners from various concentration camps, somebody in Prague had decided that additional nursing personnel were needed. A request for volunteers was issued and met with excellent response. Only a fraction of the applicants could be accepted. I don't know according to what criteria the successful applicants were selected. The fact was that only very few, if any, had any previous nursing experience.

The chief medical problems in the station were typhoid and spotty fever. Both diseases are highly contagious. The Russian command was rightfully concerned about an increase in the danger of spreading the epidemic, if untrained and undisciplined nursing personnel would come into contact with infected patients. The newcomers were therefore assigned only to auxiliary duties and were prohibited even from entering the care area of the compound. They were accommodated in one of the barracks, actually the same barracks where I had been living during my first months after deportation. There were fewer persons to the room and the three-level bunks had been replaced by single-level military ones, otherwise things were very much the same. I might add that the new group consisted exclusively of female volunteers. No former prisoners were among them and few if any had been the victims of personal persecution.

The SS guards had fled from the camp already in the week before the Russian tanks arrived. Some of them had made their way across the former border between Czechoslovakia and Germany. However, others were less lucky and had attempted to submerge and blend with the predominantly German civilian population of the "Sudetengau", annexed by Hitler in 1938.

One of these fugitives had been hunted down (I do not know exactly by whom), and returned to the camp. For whatever reasons, he ended up with his hands and feet tied together in the hands of our new nurses.

A veritable frenzy arose. He was thrown onto the floor in one of the open broad corridors of the barracks. Old straw mattresses were cut open and their contents spread on the stone plates that covered the floor in a wide circle around the poor, wretched fellow. Water was poured in places over the dry straw to prevent it from burning too fast and then the whole thing was set afire. Straw was from time to time added to replace burnt material. He was experiencing perhaps more fear than pain and soon passed out. The fire was then dampened and a pail of cold water poured over him to make him conscious again. The fire was then fanned again. The women around him had become ecstatic. A Red Army lieutenant had heard the commotion and came up to investigate. When he saw what was going on he was infuriated. "That fellow may have deserved death but not in this way. Who gave you the right to play prosecutor, judge, and executioner all in one?"

The mob was in no mood to listen. It moved threateningly against the officer and might have tried to lynch him. It retreated only when he pulled his side arm and fired some shots into the air. He then left, only to come a little later with a platoon of soldiers in full battle gear. They dispersed the crowd with rifle butts and chased them back to their lodgings.

In the meantime, nobody had guarded the fire, which had become more and more furious. The clothes of the unfortunate wretch in the centre had turned to cinders, his skin was peeling off in flakes and only a low moaning indicated that he was still alive. Judging that he was already beyond salvation, the lieutenant ordered one of his men to end his sufferings with a shot to the head. The body was then carried away and the soldiers returned to their quarters.

I observed this happening from a distance, not daring to come closer. Details I did not see are put together from the report of the lieutenant who had intervened and the story was retold to me by his commanding officer.

The experience was a shock to me. I would have understood if the former inmates of the camp had tried to exact revenge on their former tyrants. They had no firearms so they could not shoot him; perhaps they might have tried to hang him or to put him to death quickly in another way, though I am almost certain they would have rather passed him on to the military courts of the Russian army or perhaps to the local civilian authorities. I doubt very much that they would have tried to torture him to death.

Now these "nurses" had, in all likelihood, not suffered during the war more than the general deprivation. They had probably been obedient to the decrees and ordinances of the German administration and done their best to survive the war. Their frenzy, excitement, their obvious enjoyment of the sadistic torture of their helpless victim was so repulsive, so repugnant. I had heard stories about the cruelty of female members of the SS towards their prisoners, in many respects worse than their male counterparts. I certainly did not expect to see that sadistic pleasure in inflicting pain in women who had spent the war rather far from its abominations.

SENSELESS DEATH

Another incident that happened at roughly the same time, narrated to me by the two women involved.

The ghetto's electrical services department had a fairly large administrative agenda and most of the paperwork was done by female inmates. Amongst them, there were two pretty girls from Prague. After the SS had vanished, they were impatient to go home and did not want to wait for the termination of the quarantine. Before the ring of Soviet soldiers around the fortress was firmly closed, they managed to sneak out and hid in a small grove, on the side of the main road to Prague.

When the sun was setting, they ventured to the shoulder of the road, on which a continuous stream of army vehicles was rolling by. They tried to hitch a ride on one of them but with no success. Finally, an armoury jeep with two soldiers stopped and they climbed in. Unfortunately, the promised ride did not last long. After a few miles, the jeep left the road and turned into a small side road into a dark forest. There the car stopped and the girls were rather rudely asked to descend with the soldiers following them. They tore off their clothes, with the cars headlights on had their pleasure with them and then left them naked in the dark.

The soldiers had made the mistake of driving only a small distance from the highway. The lights from the almost continuous flow of traffic gave the girls the direction and naked, shivering from the cold, they stumbled back to the main road. By good fortune, a convoy of cars approached which carried the staff of the commander of the division that operated in that area.

The general, seeing in the light of his headlight two apparently naked figures at the roadside, frantically waving their arms, asked his driver to stop and sent his orderly to investigate. The girls told their story upon which the general ordered to give them some military clothes and to let them into the car. The column then sped on to the next larger town where the division was to assemble.

On arrival, he ordered all the latecomers to stand before him for inspection. Passing the rows with the girls in tow, the two rapists were soon identified. They did not even try to deny the girls' story. They had considered them legitimate spoils of war and claimed to have been generous by letting them go without killing or even injuring them.

"You know that you are no longer in enemy territory. You have received orders that what was tolerated over there would not be acceptable here. You have violated these orders and you know what the punishment for disobeying orders at the frontline is. Get rid of them as an example for all the other ones," the general thundered.

The two were led away, pale and trembling. Two shots rang out and then it was over. Addressing the girls, the general said, "You are to a degree responsible for the death of these two men. It was stupid and frivolous to venture alone at night among hordes of battle weary soldiers; some of them have not touched a female body for years. What happened to you may serve as a warning and deserved punishment. The only mitigation I can see is the time spent in the German camp. To prevent you from causing more trouble, you will stay in the female compound of the divisional jail until there is no fighting in and around Prague and a transport of our female auxiliaries going that way can take you there. Then you are on your own, and don't forget, as long as you are with us you are subject to the same disciplinary rules as everybody else."

The girls managed to come to Prague somewhat later. That their imprudent action cost two young soldiers their lives haunted them for many years to come.

* * *

EPILOGUE

The memoirs of Dr. Pollak end here. Except for the chronologically arranged stories up to his departure from Postoloprty, the memoirs are a collection of individual stories he had lived through and recollected.

While editing, some historical inaccuracies and mistakes, as well as data and names of places and persons were corrected and footnotes were added.

FROM TEREZÍN TO SASKATOON

(Dr. Pollak's memoirs cover the period ending by the liberation of Theresienstadt by the Red Army units. The final chapter was added to complement his life story. We used written materials supplied by Mrs. Mirka Pollak and available Internet sources.)

After a long quarantine, when the ghetto was hermetically sealed because of the fear of possible epidemics, Dr. Pollak could finally leave Terezín and return to Prague.

His first concern was to complete his studies at the Czech Technical University, interrupted by Germans closing all universities in November 1939. He graduated in 1946 and then served six months in the Czechoslovak army. After completing his military service, he joined the TESLA Telecommunications Company, first as a designer but soon was transferred to the research department.

In February 1948, the communist coup d´état finished the fledgling democracy and new problems emerged. In the beginning, everything looked promising and it seemed that the new regime would not bring any changes in employment, especially in research. He was wrong. His first run in with the system came in the early fifties, when he was invited to join the Communist party and flatly refused. He was never forgiven for such a sin.

He started to write a doctor's thesis and, as its topic, he chose Norbert Wiener's Information Theory. The problem was that Wiener was an American and a Jew. His theory was regarded as a capitalist aberration and Pollak's thesis was put on ice.

Then he had a stroke of luck. A well-known Soviet mathematician, Andrej Kolgomorov, came out with a theory of his own, which came to essentially the same conclusions as Wiener. When Pollak managed to obtain a copy of Kolgomorov's work he submitted it to the Dean and pointed out the analogies, the ice was broken and, after years of waiting, he received a Doctor of Technical Sciences degree in 1953.

Picture: Viktor Pollak's doctor's degree from the Czech Technical University in Prague.

In his job, he was successful, having developed a new and up-to-date communication system for the power grid, which was purchased by the Chinese government. Within the cooperation agreement, he was sent to Beijing to assist with the installation and start-up of operation. The Chinese liked his work and sent him to the Northeast to help with establishing a new energy research institute. To show their appreciation, they made him a member of an advisory committee for energy questions to the State Planning Board.

So far so good, but there was a hitch: All the other committee members were Soviet experts and they hated the idea. They tried to get rid of him by all possible means, but the Chinese did not budge. "I had the confidence of the Prime Minister, Mr. Chou En-Lai, who defended me against all attempts to discredit me." He stayed in that function for nearly two years.

Then the first signs of the Cultural Revolution began to appear and Mr.

Pollak decided to return to Czechoslovakia, although the Chinese tried to dissuade him. The way back home was more complicated. To China, he came by plane; for the return trip, he had to use the Trans-Siberian railway. For that he had to get permission from Moscow, which also arranged for the persons he was to share the compartment with, "so I would travel in politically unapproachable company," in his words. What it meant was that there would be nobody to talk with.

"When I returned to Prague, I was made to pay the price for not kow-towing to Soviets. The technical director of my institute did his best to make life miserable for me." It did not help him when he simply refused to let himself criticize his work there. After a few months, the director told him to look for another job.

Thanks to his connections with the medical community, with whom he had cooperated on medical solutions for many years, he found a job very soon, which the communists in Tesla had not expected. Not only that, he was invited to head the department of medical electronics in the Institute of Medical Technology. "I enjoyed my work there, but it did no last long. The Central Committee of the Communist Party of Czechoslovakia, perhaps upon instructions from even higher echelons, decided that the majority of educated people were anti-communist, and a Gulag-type system to re-educate them was adopted as the best solution."

The institute was dissolved and most of the technical personnel was sent "to production", in another words, to hard labour. Dr. Pollak was sentenced to underground work in the uranium mines of Jáchymov, close to the German border. Again, his connections with Prague medical community proved useful and doctors sent him with the diagnosis of nervous breakdown to a mental sanatorium far in the mountains.

As the problems in various industries multiplied, the communists began to recognize that they had blundered. His sentence was first converted to permission to work on the floor of a factory producing medical devices, and later in research, but only in a rank-and-file position.

His former institute was abolished and he was assigned to the Fuel Research Institute to work on problems of management and automation. With the communist head of his department, he made a tacit deal that he would allow Dr. Pollak to work independently and more than that, he would cover him.

The life of Dr. Pollak who, as he said, escaped death nine times, was full of strokes of luck. Some came immediately; sometimes he had to wait. One of the latter was a meeting with the husband of a Danish lady and the father of her daughter. He had met both women in Thereseienstadt and tried to help them navigate the harsh ghetto reality. They parted at the end of 1944, when the Red Cross buses evacuated all Scandinavian inmates to the neutral Sweden. He did not expect to see them ever again.

"In Prague, I used to visit the lobby of an international hotel, the only place where you could read an English newspaper. It was just the Daily Worker. One day a foreigner came to my table seeing that I was reading an English paper and asked whether he could take a seat there. He needed some information." They started to chat, and before leaving, the man introduced himself. Dr. Pollak returned the politeness remarking, "During the war I knew a lady of the same name." His new acquaintance stiffened and asked,

"Where?"

"In Theresienstadt."

"Did she have a child?"

"A small girl."

"My wife and daughter. It was you who helped them survive. We talk so often of you. Can we do something for you to show our gratitude?"

"I am afraid nothing now."

It was shortly after the 1956 Hungarian uprising and the internal situation in Czechoslovakia was extremely tense. The man said that he came every year to Prague on business, and if he could have his address, he would get in touch.

In the subsequent years, they met several times, but it was not until the mid-sixties when Dr. Pollak asked him directly, "I would like to get out of here. Can you help me?"

"I can't promise anything, but I will try," was the response.

Two years passed without any contact and he thought the man had forgotten. Then he received a letter with the address label of the King of Denmark and an invitation to accept a position as a Visiting Scientist at the Technical University of Denmark in Lyngby. With the letter, he went to the passport office of the state security police. Perhaps they were embarrassed to reject the king's invitation and he got the passport and exit permit. On the eve of departure, he married Mirka and together they left.

In Denmark, they stayed for two years, but the university had no permanent position and it was time to look for one. To return was out of the question because, in the meantime, the Soviets had invaded Czechoslovakia. He addressed a number of universities in Canada and the United States applying for a job and the first positive reply came from the University of Saskatchewan in Saskatoon, Canada. "I accepted it and have never regretted it."

Finally, Dr. Pollak could fully put to use his scientific potential. He started as an Associate Professor of Electrical Engineering and soon was promoted to full Professor. Most of his time between 1970 and 1984, he was devoted to the Division of Biomedical Engineering, which he had helped establish. Under his leadership, it became one of the largest departments of its kind in Canada and soon acquired both a national and an international reputation. Scholars from many European, South American and Asian countries, as well as from Canada, were coming to work in the Division because they considered it an honour to cooperate with such an expert in biomedical engineering, who used his wide spectrum of expertise in several areas of engineering to employ the latest cutting-edge electronic technologies in medicine.

We have mentioned that in 1984 he had retired. However, he continued to work as Professor Emeritus at his home university and as Visiting Honourary Professor at the University of Aachen in Germany until 1995.

Dr. Pollak loved travelling and, except for the Arctic and Antarctica there are very few countries on this earth that he had not seen. He passed away after a brief illness on one of his trips on April 29th, 1999.

His memory, though, lives on, and not only in patents and inventions. Viktor and Mirka Pollak established a scholarship at the University of Saskatchewan for students pursuing graduate or postdoctoral studies in the fields of biomedical engineering, neurology, rehabilitation engineering or cardiology instrumentation. Nor will he be forgotten at the University of Aachen, where the Prize of Viktor and Mirka Pollak for doctoral and master theses in biomedical engineering is awarded annually since 2004.

Viktor und Mirka Pollak-Preis für Medizinische Technik 2010

Viktor and Mirka Pollak Award for Biomedical Engineering 2010

Springorum-Denkmünze
Borchersplaketten
Viktor und Mirka Pollak
Preis
Preisträger
F.C. Trapp-Preis
Eugen Piriet Preis
Ludwig von
Bogdandy-Preis

Mit dem Viktor und Mirka Pollak-Preis werden herausragende Abschlussarbeiten in der Elektrotechnik und Informationstechnik, die eine medizinisch-technische Problemstellung behandeln, ausgezeichnet. Der Preis wird bestimmungsgemäß aus dem **Viktor und Mirka Pollak-Fonds für medizinische Technik** finanziert, der der Förderung interdisziplinärer medizintechnischer Forschung gewidmet ist.

Der Fonds wurde im Jahre 2004 von Frau Mirka Pollak gestiftet. Er gilt dem Vermächtnis Ihres Ehegatten **Viktor Pollak**, der in den Jahren von 1968 bis kurz vor seinem Tode 1999 an der University of Saskatchewan in Saskatoon, Kanada, Pionierarbeit auf dem Gebiet „Biomedical Engineering" geleistet hat.

Im Sinne des Stifters werden an eine auszeichnungswürdige Diplomarbeit oder Masterarbeit neben einer überdurchschnittlichen Benotung die folgenden Auswahlkriterien angelegt:

• Die Arbeit soll auf dem Gebiet der Elektrotechnik und Informationstechnik angesiedelt sein und eine medizinisch-technische Problemstellung behandeln. Es muss sich um eine aus Sicht der Medizin relevante Aufgabe handeln.

• Die Arbeit muss sich mit der Problemstellung zugrunde liegenden medizinischen Anwendung auseinandersetzen. Sie soll auch für Fachgebietsfremde verständlich geschrieben sein.

• Die darin erarbeitete Lösung soll innovativen Charakter haben. Das Potential zur klinischen Umsetzung soll klar erkennbar sein.

• Die technische Umsetzung des bearbeiteten Forschungsansatzes muss im Vordergrund stehen.

• Die Arbeit wurde innerhalb des Zeitraumes Wintersemesters 2008/2009 bis Sommersemesters 2010 abgeschlossen.

Anstelle einer Diplomarbeit oder Masterarbeit kann der Preis auch für den detailliert ausgearbeiteten Arbeitsvorschlag eines Promotionsprojektes oder für eine außergewöhnliche Bachelorarbeit, die sich in Qualität und Umfang an diesen Kriterien messen lassen können, verliehen werden.

Der Preis wird seit dem Jahr 2005 jährlich ausgeschrieben. Für das Jahr 2010 ist er mit 1.000 € dotiert. Er wird auf dem Tag der Elektrotechnik und Informationstechnik verliehen.

Die Auswahl der Preisträger erfolgt durch ein Kuratorium, dem der Dekan der Fakultät für Elektrotechnik und Informationstechnik der RWTH Aachen, ein Fachvertreter der Medizintechnik aus dieser Fakultät, ein der Technik nahestehendes Mitglied der Medizinischen Fakultät sowie ein Mitglied des Vorstandes der Freunde und Förderer der RWTH Aachen e.V. (proRWTH) angehören. Das Kuratorium wird derzeit koordiniert durch Prof. Dr.-Ing. Dietrich Meyer-Ebrecht, Lehrstuhl für Bildverarbeitung der RWTH, eMail *meyer-ebrecht@rwth-aachen.de*.

Vorschläge für auszeichnungswürdige Arbeiten bitten wir formlos mit einer kurzen Laudatio der betreuenden Lehrstuhlinhaberin bzw. des betreuenden Lehrstuhlinhabers und einem Exemplar der Arbeit bis zum 30. September 2010 an den **Koordinator** einzureichen.

Viktor and Mirka Pollak Prize for outstanding doctoral and master theses in biomedical engineering.

Certificate of the Czechoslovak Ministry of Defence issued to political prisoners.

September 1998

Dear Viktor

We extend to you Viktor our most sincere congratulations on the honour and recognition which you recently received from the medical profession for your many contributions to the field of biomedical engineering, as a researcher and as the Head of the Biomedical Engineering Division at the University of Saskatchewan. It is an honour of which you should be very proud. You took this Division from one little known in the country to one with an international recognition. Your personal research was and still is of international repute. Congratulations on a job very, very well done.

Eugenie and Peter

Letter of appreciation

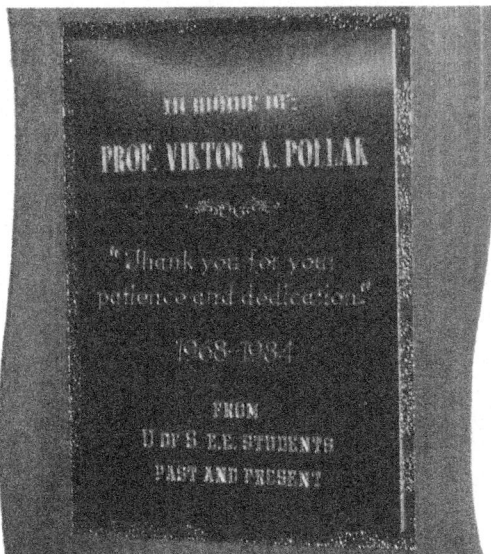

Award by students of electrical engineering

PRESENTED TO

DR. VIKTOR POLLAK

IN APPRECIATION
OF YOUR SERVICE TO THE
HEALTH OF THE PEOPLE
OF SASKATOON

CPSIA information can be obtained at www.ICGtesting.com
Printed in the USA
LVOW04s1914261214

420479LV00007B/97/P